STORMTROOPER
ON THE
EASTERN FRONT

STORMTROOPER

ON THE

EASTERN FRONT

Fighting with Hitler's Latvian SS

Mintauts Blosfelds

edited by

Lisa Blosfelds

Pen & Sword
MILITARY

First published in Great Britain in 2008 by
Pen & Sword Military
an imprint of
Pen & Sword Books Ltd
47 Church Street
Barnsley
South Yorkshire
S70 2AS

ISBN 978 1 84415 720 4

Printed and bound in England by
Biddles Ltd, King's Lynn

Pen & Sword Books Ltd incorporates the imprints of Pen & Sword
Aviation, Pen & Sword Maritime, Pen & Sword Military, Wharncliffe
Local History, Pen & Sword Select, Pen & Sword Military Classics and
Leo Cooper.

For a complete list of Pen & Sword titles please contact
PEN & SWORD BOOKS LIMITED
47 Church Street, Barnsley, South Yorkshire, S70 2AS, England
E-mail: enquiries@pen-and-sword.co.uk
Website: www.pen-and-sword.co.uk

Contents

Maps

Foreword and Acknowledgements

This book comprises an edited version of an account my father wrote of life in Latvia and his experiences in the Latvian Legion during the Second World War. The parts omitted comprise: a lengthy account of life in Latvia under the first occupation of the country by the Russians, and during the German occupation before my father was old enough to be called up to serve in the armed forces (these parts would have made the book about half as long again had they been included): material only likely to be of interest to our family or unlikely to be of interest to the military reader; material which is duplicated; and small details such as astronomical observations made by my father, whose hobby was astronomy as a young man.

In addition, I have made minor amendments to spelling, grammar and wording, and have added occasional footnotes to clarify certain points. Anyone wishing to consult a full copy of the typescript will find one at the Imperial War Museum and another at The Second World War Experience in Leeds, both of whom have kindly accepted copies for their archives.

I would like to thank Dr Peter Liddle of The Second World War Experience for his advice on getting the memoirs finished, Brigadier Henry Wilson for his help and encouragement in dealing with the typescript, my editor, Bobby Gainher, for his kindness, patience, support and helpful suggestions, and my employer, Robert Johnson, without whose kindness and generosity in the use of the computer and photocopier this book would never have been published.

Lisa Blosfelds

Notes on the Pronunciation
of Latvian Names

Latvian is a phonetically written language. However, certain sounds are pronounced differently to how they are spelt in English.

'AU' is pronounced 'OW' in Latvian, hence my father's name is properly pronounced MINTOWTS (although he was known as 'Min' when he came to England) and the River Daugava on which Riga stands is pronounced DOWGAVA rather than DORGAVA. 'AI' is pronounced 'EYE', so that his girlfriend's name is properly 'GYDA'. 'IE' is pronounced 'EAR' so that his comrade's name was pronounced 'LEARPER'. In addition, 'INS' at the end of the name is pronounced 'INSH' and, in common with most Eastern European languages, 'J' is pronounced as 'Y', as in year.

Biographical Note

My father was born on his father's family farm near Jelgava in Latvia on 16 April 1924. His father, Arturs Blosfelds, was a lecturer in mathematics at the local secondary school and his mother, Lilija Gerbers, was one of his students. He was twenty-eight and she twenty-two when they married. Just before my father was four years old his father died while being operated on for a stomach ulcer. By that time he had two younger sisters. His mother had to go to work in Riga, leaving her children to be brought up on the family farm, although they later joined her in Riga for the sake of their education. My grandmother would have liked my father to have had a career in the diplomatic corps, but the war intervened and he spent the time between leaving school and being conscripted working in a motorcycle workshop and on the farm.

After the war, along with many Latvians, my father was allowed to come to England on condition that he worked for a while in the coal mines. He arrived in Lowestoft in 1947 and was posted to Doncaster. There he was billeted in a former Bevin Boys hostel where my mother was working in the canteen. They married in 1951. I was born in 1959 and am an only child.

After leaving the pit, where he had worked in transport rather than at the coalface, my father found work with a company which made agricultural machinery where several other Latvians were also employed. He worked initially in the foundry but was later promoted to the offices. With the firm cutting down on its employees, he took early retirement at the age of fifty-five. He died in 1987 at the age of sixty-three of lung cancer.

My father was 6ft tall and had black hair, grey eyes and a strong athletic body until his final illness. Having learned some English at school, he quickly became fluent in the language, speaking and writing it better than many local people. I was never aware of any accent, though others did say that they could hear a certain foreign intonation in his speech. In later years he even became quite hesitant in the use of his native tongue as he was not one to socialize much with the other Latvians who had settled in Doncaster.

Having been raised on a farm, my father was very capable with his hands. He had a workshop in our garden where he spent a great deal of time making things. Among these was a spinning wheel which he made for me from scratch; he restored an antique clock which he found in a ditch in our woods; and he designed and made himself a tent which he sewed together completely by hand. He also made himself a telescope using some lenses which he 'organized' from the periscope of a German submarine while working in Hamburg docks as a Displaced Person. Despite being colour blind, he painted in oils, usually Latvian landscapes. In later years he was a great hiker, completing many long-distance walks such as the Yorkshire coast, Cleveland Way and Lyke Wake Walk, as well as the Pennine Way, and made most of the equipment which he carried with him. While walking the Pennine Way he camped one night at Top Withens, which led him to read *Wuthering Heights* and then to becoming a member of the Brontë Society. He spent a great deal of time after his retirement walking in Brontë country, comparing the real-life landscape with that of the novels, and had a couple of articles on the subject published in *Pennine* magazine. His Brontë research has been placed in the Brotherton Library of Leeds University.

In 1989 one of my father's sisters, along with her daughter-in-law and granddaughter, were allowed to come and visit us. She brought with her some soil from the family plot in Latvia which she placed on my father's grave.

Lisa Blosfelds

Introduction

When Germany attacked Russia on 22 June 1941, the people of Latvia had been under Russian Communist rule for a whole year, during which time they had experienced Communism in action. Even the few Latvians, who in the beginning of this period had had some hope of a better life, were bitterly disappointed. Within a year the country had become poor and the people were terrified of their new rulers. Many of them had been arrested and disappeared without trace. There were rumours circulating everywhere of the tortures meted out by the Russian Secret Police on those who fell into their hands. Anyone still believing the Russian propaganda of a better life just around the corner suffered the final disillusionment on 14 June 1941. In one night the Russians arrested some 15,000 persons, loaded them onto cattle trucks and deported these wholly innocent people to the concentration camps of Russia. The total number of children and adults killed and deported in one year by the Communists amounted to almost 36,000. Nearly everyone in Latvia lost a relative or member of their family.

When the German Army reached Riga in a swift ten-day advance after the start of the war, they were greeted as liberators and welcomed by the people. Only then did the full horror of the Communist rule become known. Mass graves of tortured victims were opened up, and lists of arrested people and instruments of physical torture were found at the Secret Police headquarters in Riga.

Latvian men who had a personal score to settle with the Russians volunteered for service on the German side straight away and formed the first units of Latvians fighting in the Second World War. They were employed in actions against Red partisans in Russia and manned the front line near Leningrad.

By the time the real Latvian Legion was formed in 1943, the people had become disappointed with their new masters and their

1

arrogant behaviour; all the volunteers had already gone and joined in the fighting. The German Army was on the defensive in the East and in the hope of getting willing helpers, Adolf Hitler ordered the formation of a Latvian Legion in one of his directives.

The German rulers of Latvia, as part of their efforts towards a total war, decided to put this order into effect at the beginning of February 1943. A decree was issued ordering all Latvian men born between the years 1919 to 1924 to report to their labour exchanges for duty with military units and work important for the war. The legal basis for this decree was the order of 19 December 1941. Issued by the German minister for occupied eastern regions, Alfred Rosenberg, this concerned the duty of obligatory work. From the military viewpoint this call-up affected the most valuable part of the Latvian nation. The total number liable to be called to serve was estimated to be in the region of 90,000, although the Germans were realistic and calculated that they could realize only some 58,000 men at the most. They decided to allocate the new recruits as follows: 25,000 in work units with the German Army, 15–17,000 in the Latvian Legion, 6,000 as Auxiliary troops with the police and security units, and 10,000 in work important to the war effort.

On 26 February 1943, the labour exchanges of Latvia started the call-up examinations. Call-up was initially considered to be on a voluntary basis. After a medical examination the men were asked to decide with which unit they would like to serve, and to sign a form stating that they had volunteered for service.

The Latvian local authorities had resisted the intended call-up for some time and had questioned the legality of the whole concept of such an action. On seeing that the Germans did not take any notice of their arguments, the Latvian administrators wrote once more to the German High Commissioner asking for a number of concessions.

The main reason why the local government organizations co-operated in the call-up was that the Red Army was once more approaching the borders of Latvia and Latvians wished to keep the Communists out of the country at any price. In the meantime, they hoped for more favourable treatment from the German side and expected a political settlement after the war which would still recognize Latvia as an independent state.

The main fighting units of the Legion were two divisions: the

19th Division (19 Waffen-Grenadier Division der SS, Lett. Nr 2), and the 15th Division (15 Waffen-Grenadier Division der SS, Lett. Nr 1). Each division consisted of three regiments of some 3,000 men each. Beside the six regiments there were artillery and other units of the Latvian Legion.

Initially the 19th Division consisted mainly of volunteers and was already at the front line in 1942 near Leningrad. The 15th Division was formed as a result of the call-up of 1943, the first units arriving at the front line that same summer. This division was almost completely destroyed in the retreat from Russia in summer 1944. In the autumn of the same year, the 15th Division was sent to Germany to be re-equipped and trained, and remained there until the end of the war. The 19th Division stayed at the front line in Courland until the capitulation in May 1945. These men fought valiantly and the Division was mentioned several times in German Army reports. From the autumn of 1944 the Courland peninsula remained cut off as the Russians tried to take it with superior forces, but failed because of the stubborn resistance of the defenders.

I served in the ranks of the Latvian Legion for nearly two years, followed by another eleven months in prisoner-of-war camps. During this time I was in dangerous situations many times but managed to survive. The greatest danger, as far as I was concerned, was falling into the hands of our enemies, the Russians. I found that the waiting was the most tiring and nerve-racking part of our duties, while the following actions were comparatively easy and exciting.

Mintauts Blosfelds
Doncaster, 30 January 1965

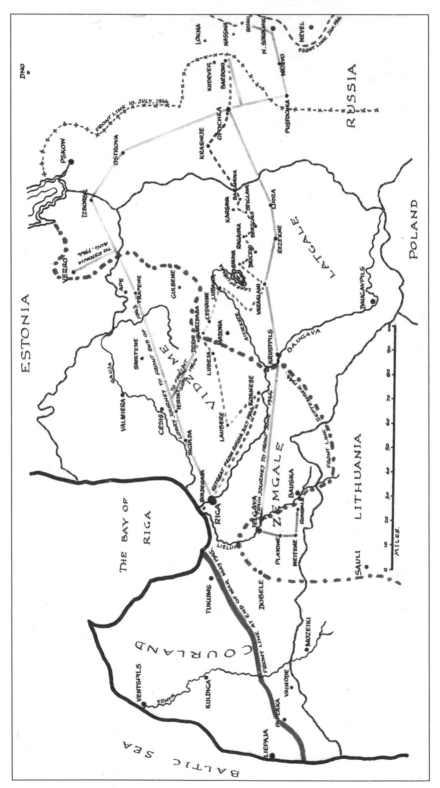

Latvia

Part I

Training

Chapter 1

How the German Army Entered Latvia in the Late Summer of 1941

On the afternoon of 30 June 1941 noises of firing and explosions could be heard somewhere in the distance and though they did not get any nearer, for safety's sake we remained in the cellar of our house. I was sitting on the cellar steps reading my book on astronomy, when I was suddenly startled by powerful banging on the front door. The caretaker's wife hurried to open the door and we saw outside, standing in the street, soldiers dressed in strange uniforms. They were the first Germans who, coming along Nometnu Street, had just reached our house. The soldiers were thirsty and asked for a drink. One of the women brought a bucket of water and a cup. The Germans drank and thanked her, then went out into the street. They did not go any further towards Riga along Slokas Street, but stood at the crossing for a while talking. Then they fired a rocket into the sky and went away, returning the way they had come. We were very surprised by the visit of these Germans as we had not thought it possible they could be so near already. The silence up until then had made us think that the Germans had perhaps been thrown back from the approaches to Riga. I made a note of this historic moment by writing on the title page of my book with a pencil in fine letters: '1941. 30. 6. 20h 30m. FIRST GERMANS IN RIGA.'

Now we were not sure whether the Germans had retreated, or just moved back to await reinforcements in order to clear our neighbourhood of Communists. Somehow we did not believe they had retreated altogether. After a while the noise of battle restarted and approached us from the direction of the Square of Victory, becoming louder all the time. The noise culminated in several very powerful blasts which resulted in our front door being blown open, breaking all the glass in it when it hit the inside wall. The next moment new German soldiers appeared. A group of them, armed with rifles and sub-machine guns, ran through the open door to our block of flats. From the staircase they roughly pushed all male persons out into the street, me among them. Then they began to search through the building and send out any other men found inside. We were being arrested for only a short time, the Germans explained to my mother in response to her anxious questions, and after a check of our documents we would be released and allowed to return home. It seemed that they were searching for Soviet soldiers dressed in civilian clothes among us.

By now the Germans were coming along Slokas Street from the direction of the Square of Victory in single file along both sides of the street. They did not walk in the middle of the street, which would have been most difficult in any case because of the tram wires and rubble there. While the building was being searched, I and others had to wait in Nometnu Street in a column, which gave me ample opportunity to study our new rulers.

The Germans were all young and looked efficient. They behaved with assurance, and it appeared they were well trained in the art of war; the first impression was altogether favourable. They had rolled up the sleeves and opened the necks on their field grey jackets. I noticed especially a dark-skinned lad who, leaning on a machine gun, stood near the wall of our house. He was either tired from battle or a phlegmatic character. All the time I observed him his expression never changed. The eyes of this German looked somewhere in the far distance and he seemed so deep in thought that even he did not notice what was happening around him.

When the searchers returned to the street, a command was given and our column of men began to march, guarded by a few Germans, towards the Market of Agenskalns. Further on we turned to the left and reached the edge of the Square of Victory near Barinu Street. Here we had to wait for about a quarter of an hour – it seemed that the Germans themselves did not know what to do with us. Eventually we were marched off, moving once more into the

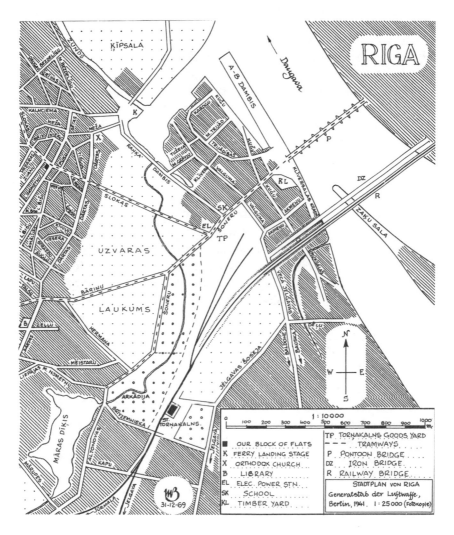

streets of Agenskalns, and reached the end of our journey in a school yard surrounded by a high fence made of wooden boards. The Germans had already made themselves at home in the school building, the entrance of which was guarded by an armed sentry. Another soldier stood guard by the gate in the street.

Meanwhile, a warm and still summer night had darkened around us. The people who had been arrested together walked slowly, making endless rounds of the fence. Groups of friends and acquaintances assembled here and there discussing recent events and future expectations. I did not know anyone in the yard and had to walk around it on my own waiting for the morning. Although no one knew what the next day might bring, nobody seemed to worry about it, nevertheless preparing for the possible check of documents. Quite soon torn up pieces of paper appeared in the corners of the school yard – Communist Party membership cards and Latvian passports recording the owner's attendance at Communist courses and lectures. By morning light such papers littered the whole yard.

Towards breakfast time a crowd of women assembled outside the gates. Somehow they had got to know of our whereabouts and now came to visit us and bring some food and drink. My mother had arrived to see me and bring me something to eat. She already knew enough to tell me that we would be released towards midday.

Waiting for our release – looking through a gap in the boards of the fence – I could watch the activities of the German soldiers on the street. One of their units was just resting on the other side of the street. The soldiers either sat on the ground or on their rucksacks, eating soup out of mess tins, drinking and smoking cigars. I could sense that their spirits were high after the victory at Riga. After watching the Germans for a while I began once more to circle the yard when I heard music. The melody was at the same time familiar and strange because I had not heard it for some time.

'God Bless Latvia' – the national anthem – echoed from a tall building, coming from a wireless set placed in a wide-open window. The Germans had already occupied the broadcasting house! Hearing the anthem, people stopped walking, turned towards the sound and stood still. Hats were removed from heads and the crowd stood quietly listening. The anthem was followed by an announcement about the freeing of Riga from the Bolsheviks, thanks to the armed forces of Germany, but by now a noise of excited voices in the yard drowned out the sound coming from the radio. Soon afterwards the gates were opened wide and we were free to go.

Arriving home, I was greeted by my mother who had prepared a meal while waiting for me. During the meal she told me about the things that had happened while I had been absent. A group of Red Army soldiers, or local Communists, had barricaded themselves into the cellar of a house on the corner of Puku Street. Through the windows of the cellar they had opened fire on the Germans approaching from the Square of Victory and had probably killed some of them. The Germans had pulled back and had begun to mortar the house until the Reds had surrendered or been killed. The terrible bangs ending the battle during the night had been the explosions of mortar bombs. As a result of this bombardment the roof of the house was now blown away and all the windows were blackened by smoke. Otherwise the night had passed quietly. The Germans had not approached our house any more, but to feel more secure my mother had spent the night in Mrs Zade's flat.

I could not rest at home. I wanted to see with my own eyes the damage caused by the war in our neighbourhood, and went out. First I walked along Nometnu Street towards the Agenskalns landing stage. Going along the Ranka Dambis towards Riga, I came to the stream which flows through the Square of Victory and into the bay there. Crossing the bridge over the stream I saw the first dead of the Red Army. It appeared they had taken refuge below the banks and had been surprised there by the Germans. More motionless bodies lay on the sandhill across the stream and near the other bridge on Slokas Street towards the park of Arkadija. Following the stream I crossed the sandy open space and on reaching Slokas Street came into a real kingdom of death. Several Red soldiers had fallen near the bridge and some of them were even under it. Nearby lay one dead soldier who, in the agony of his death, had scratched deep marks in the sand leaving a mark of his suffering. Now his hand was covered by buzzing flies. A whole row of dead soldiers lay along the Slokas Street bank facing south. These appeared to have taken up a position in a small depression between the bridge and the electricity sub-station on the corner of Soneru Street. Here they had been surprised by the Germans or died while holding out to the last man. In the warm sunshine I could smell them – they were covered with flies and I did not feel like examining them any closer.

Returning to the Ranka Dambis, I reached the corner of Soneru Street. Directly on the street corner pavement lay one Red soldier with a shattered skull. Here bodies could be seen in great numbers, several of them with injuries similar to the last one. I thought it possible that these soldiers had been shot when surrendering to the Germans. I had heard that a bullet in the forehead shatters the skull when emerging from the back of the head, especially if fired from a close distance.

Soneru Street, from the Tornakalns goods yard to the pontoon bridge, was full of burnt-out lorries, carts, field guns and other weapons, dead horses and soldiers. Some of the dead bodies hung from ammunition carts or the cabs of lorries. Their clothing had been burned and they looked like charred chunks of meat. Some buildings on the northern side of Soneru Street were still burning. Both sides of the street were so full of rubbish and debris that a passage was possible only along the middle of the street, climbing over discarded equipment and dead soldiers. It appeared that these Reds had been trying to get to the bridge but, finding it blown up, had become jammed in the street. The Germans coming from the direction of Tornakalns had arrived, surprised the hopelessly crowded Red soldiers and had shot them all. From the direction of Riga came the sound of a few shots and a couple of bullets cracked overhead. I did not go right up to the bridge, but turned back and went along Soneru Street where I met two German officers. Carrying cameras on straps around their necks, they came towards the bridge chatting gaily – evidently well satisfied by the course of events.

Returning home, I met a column of marching Germans turning from Slokas Street into Nometnu Street. They marched in an assertive manner and sang 'Lebe wohl du kleine Monika'. Yes, now they had a full right to march and sing – all Riga belonged to them.

Latvian nationalists could breathe freely once more. A group of them appeared on Slokas Street, dressed in the uniforms of the Latvian Army and Home Guard. All of them had red-white-red armbands and they marched off along the street towards Riga.

The part of the city called Old Riga had suffered heavily during the action. All the old houses around the ancient Mansion House, and from there to the river, had burned down and crumbled to rubble. Among the notable buildings lost were the House of the Blackheaded and the Mansion House, which had housed a valuable library of old and irreplaceable books. Many buildings in Old Riga were damaged and the narrow streets were full of rubble. In some of the streets I saw anti-aircraft guns with their barrels pointing to the sky, just as they had been left by the Russians. The smell of burning and decay filled the air. In several places I saw small heaps of plaster, the only remains of many busts of Stalin. Not long before these busts had adorned the rooms of various state offices. After the German entry into Riga the busts had been thrown out of windows and smashed on the pavements, so expressing the people's disgust with the former ruler and his system.

The famous wooden spire of St Peter's Church had fallen victim to the flames and the copper cockerel which had stood on top of the spire now lay, large as a horse, in the forecourt. I saw it there, flame blackened and broken by the fall from a great height. The crypt under the church had been opened by a big gap in the collapsed church wall, and through the gap I could see old-fashioned coffins in several layers. A great crowd of people had assembled here to view the damage done to the most famous church in Riga.

Chapter 2

Life under German Occupation, 1941 to 1943

An order came one day that all Red Army equipment and weapons must be handed in at the Council House – they were still being found in the forests and fields, abandoned by their owners while fleeing east. From Bemberi[1] we delivered a whole cart-load of weapons, but we did not give them all up. We kept one brand-new automatic rifle, covered it in oil and wrapped it in a tarred sack. Then we buried the rifle, along with some ammunition, in a dry place on the bank of the garden pond. We also concealed some hand grenades in hollow trees and hid whole clips of rifle ammunition behind the beams of the old house.

By now the rationing of food and other goods was being introduced even in country districts. We received only a little paraffin for use in oil lamps, and were always short of it, particularly as we had to save the paraffin for use in storm lanterns when going to the stables and cow shed in the evening. In the house we often used a radio accumulator and one small flashlight bulb. This gave very little light, but paraffin was in such short supply that we had to manage without lighting the oil lamp. We lacked horseshoes and the nails for attaching them. These particular items were brought to us by German Army soldiers, in black market exchange for bacon, eggs and butter. One of their horse transport units was stationed at Svete and they were also able to supply tobacco and cigarettes in exchange for food.

Call-up

Life at the technical college of Jelgava passed in a quiet and orderly manner, but there was excitement among the older pupils that spring when they all received small postcards ordering them to appear before a medical commission on 18 March before being called up into the armed forces. Punishment was threatened for those who did not keep the appointment. The postcards were sent to all those born in 1924 or earlier, and I received my order on a Saturday. When I told my landlady about my call-up she seemed quite upset, but I did not mind at all. I rather looked forward to some adventure and a change in my life.

On 18 March the medical examination started at 9.00 a.m. and was held in the house next to the one where I rented my room. First of all we had to fill in a form giving our birth dates, illnesses we had had, parentage and so on. After that we were examined thoroughly by several doctors and told to go to a large room and wait there. At one end of this room there was a long table behind which sat Latvian and German officers. We were called to stand before them one by one and were asked whether we would prefer to serve with the Latvian Legion or to be enrolled into the German Army as helpers and engineers. I had not heard anything good about service with the Germans and therefore decided to join the Latvian Legion. We were told to sign a declaration saying that we were joining as volunteers, and then allowed to go home. We were also told that we would be notified in due course where and when to report for service. One of the new recruits would not sign the declaration and the officers tried to talk him into signing. They even threatened him with punishment, but in the end let him go saying it did not matter – he would have to report for service in any case.

It seems that the Russians did not get hold of these documents after the war. If they had acquired the 'voluntary' declarations, they could have demanded our handing over from the Western Powers as collaborators and helpers in the German war effort.

About a week after the medical examination I received my orders to report for service at Paplaka on 12 May 1943. The only thing I had to take with me was enough food for three days – nothing else was required.

Our special recruits' train left Jelgava at 7.00 a.m. travelling towards the west. A German soldier sat in the seat opposite to me and I tried out my German language by asking him about service in the armed forces. The man told me we would be trained for about three months, then we would get one month's leave, and only after that could we expect to be sent to the front.

Around dinner time we reached Mozeiki in Lithuania and were surprised to see a large crowd of black marketeers in the station yard. In Latvia such dealings had to be done secretly, but here everything could be bought quite openly. This pleased the lads from the next compartment – they had been drinking since Jelgava and had just finished their last bottle. Now they had an opportunity to acquire 'Lithuanian Moonshine' – a potent illicit spirit distilled from potatoes and rye. The buyers tested every bottle before paying for it. One could not trust the foreigners and they did not wish to purchase a weak brew or pure water.

Soon we continued on our way, singing and shouting the whole way, and arrived at Paplaka late in the afternoon. A couple of uniformed Legionnaires were waiting for us at the station and we followed them in a disorderly column along the railway embankment to the manor of Paplaka. The 2-mile walk was difficult for those who had been drinking, but with the help of friends even they managed to keep up with the rest, and we all eventually reached our destination.

At the gates of the manor we were greeted by the Regimental Commander, Kripens. He was already dressed in full SS uniform and greeted us in German fashion with a raised hand. We did not take too much notice of him. His theatrical appearance called forth only suppressed laughter and merriment. The yard of the manor was soon filled with new recruits, and then we were told to go into a building to spend the night.

I entered a large room which was full of bunk beds. Each of these had a straw-filled mattress but no blankets. After climbing onto a top bed I was preparing to have some supper when two men entered the room carrying a large container of coffee. I was very thirsty and glad to have something to drink, but soon discovered that the coffee was black and bitter. It did not contain any milk or sugar and was made with the German substitute which I had not yet learned to like.

When I went outside later the sun had just set. The western

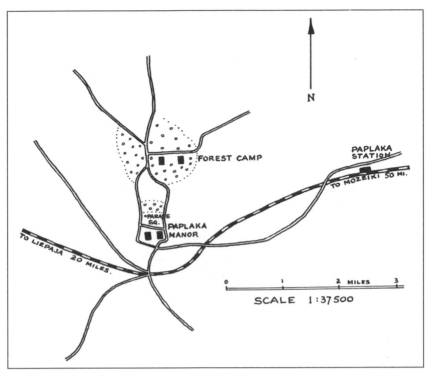

Paplaka Manor

horizon was glowing red and it had become cooler all of a sudden. I could feel the approach of night. Directly across the yard I could see an old house, the main building of the old manor. The building in which I was to spend the night was of a much later date, built for soldiers and correspondingly appointed. There were altogether three such barracks in Paplaka – two in the forest camp and one in the manor yard. The barracks had been built for the Red Army garrison of 1939–1940 which was stationed here in accordance with the agreement between Latvia and the Soviet Union concluded in 1939. The soldiers' quarters were primitive. In the lavatories there were no separate compartments, only a row of holes on a raised concrete platform. Each storey of the building had one large room where one company slept in three-tier bunks. A long corridor that ran along one end of the room was used for storing rifles on weapon stands. Two small rooms, one at each end of the corridor, served as quarters for the Company Commander and the Company Office.

Everything was quiet now; with only a nightingale was still singing somewhere in the bushes surrounding the manor. In one corner of the yard a group of new recruits was talking quietly to some Ukrainian policemen who were quartered in the old manor house across the yard. The Latvians were trying to find out where they could obtain something stronger than coffee. After acquiring the information they needed they departed into the night, and I could hear their comment: 'Tonight we are still free, let tomorrow look after itself!'

I sat down on the cool grass and smoked a cigarette. Here I was, for the first time in my life separated from home and my own people. What would the future bring? A question without an answer. Strange place, strange people and I had to look after myself. The night was quite dark when I tossed away the cigarette butt and went inside. I laid down fully clothed and went to sleep listening to the sound of a guitar played by a Latgallian recruit.

Notes
1 A farm belonging to the family. (*LB*)

Chapter 3

Paplaka Recruit Training Depot, May to July 1943

The next morning we were awakened with the sun and told to stand in the yard so that we could be assigned to our companies. This took some time. Everyone was asked his name, occupation, education and other things. Our answers were noted down by the clerks, and the officers told us to go across the yard and join our companies. It was very cold for standing about and waiting – during the night a keen frost had covered the ground with a glittering deposit. Although the sun was shining, we were still in the shadow of the building and could not feel its warmth. The unit to which I was sent was the 9th Company of the 3rd Battalion. This was the instructors' company, and to get into it one had to be tall, with higher than primary education. It was intended to prepare instructors from the men in the 9th Company for the Regiment's needs. I was glad to leave the cold manor yard and start the 2-mile walk to the forest barracks where we were to live. We walked quickly to warm ourselves in the bright sunshine, reached our destination and halted to await further orders.

There, in the middle of the leafy forest, were two barrack blocks, similar to the one at Paplaka manor. We sat at the roadside for about an hour awaiting the return of the soldiers who had shown us the way. The sun was warm and we were beginning to feel sleepy when they came back. This time we were told to stand in front of the 3rd Battalion building and the Company Sergeant Major made a list of our names. He was a young lad, just like ourselves, but it was rumoured that he had already been to the front in Russia. We were then dismissed to await further orders.

The Company assembled anew at about 2.00 p.m., this time having to stand on the road which led past our barracks. The Sergeant Major checked our names against his list and went to report to the Company Commander, returning with him a little while later.

The Company Commander was a thinnish, middle-aged officer with the rank of Captain. A characteristic feature of his were his dark, piercing eyes which seemed to demand instant obedience. After a swift glance at his new company the officer made a short speech. He introduced himself as Captain Pommers and added that we, as potential instructors could expect particularly strict discipline. A long time was spent in arranging us by our height in a line. Then the Company was split into sections and platoons, and the commanders of these were selected from among us. Section after section went to the stores to be issued with uniforms, boots and other equipment. There was a great shortage of large boots, so that after a couple of weeks some fully uniformed soldiers were still wearing shoes.

That evening we were assembled again on the road for the 10.00 p.m. roll call. We looked more like soldiers now, but a few of us had some buttons undone or the eagle on the belt buckle had its talons pointing upwards. These things were corrected by the Sergeant Major on his walk down the line. He took another good look at us, and then disgustedly went to report to the Company Commander. When the officer arrived there were a few minutes left before 10 o'clock, and he spent this time inspecting us and correcting our uniforms. Exactly at 10 we were ordered to stand to attention and sing 'God Bless Latvia' followed by 'The Great Lord is our Saviour', after which we said the Lord's Prayer. The command 'At ease!' followed and then the Sergeant Major read out the order of duties for the next day. Only then were we released for the night.

Although we had been told to be in our beds by 10.30 and to be quiet, this order was not observed. A large crowd of recruits had assembled in the free space between the bed ends and the corridor. Somebody played an accordion, others stood around him singing and beating time. In a quieter moment loud shouts were heard from the periphery of the crowd and a thin, dark youth started to push his way through the spectators. He was naked except for a towel around his hips which did not hide much. On reaching the middle of the crowd he began to dance a wild, nude jig urged on by loud yells and raucous laughter. The noise, of course, was instantly noticed by the Company Sergeant Major, who ran into the room followed by the night duty man. A couple of shouts from the Sergeant Major sent us all scurrying to our beds, but the matter did not end there. The night duty man had to suffer for reporting to the Sergeant Major. Blasphemous curses were aimed at him from all around, water poured on him from the top bunks, and it was late in the night before we quietened down. Only then could I hear the rhythmic steps of the guard outside and the snoring and grunting of my new comrades in their sleep.

The next six weeks at Paplaka passed quickly. Every day we learned the art of marching. We got up with the sun and after breakfast began the unending marching, turning and singing. Some of the more uncoordinated recruits found great difficulty in acquiring the necessary speed and adroitness, and yet after a couple of weeks we could march quite well to the obvious delight of our commander. Field training was more to our liking. We went out into the country, learned to read maps and use a compass. The theoretical art of war was explained to us while we sat at the long dinner tables in front of our barracks. We had some night training, were taught how to approach the enemy quietly, how to tell direction by the Pole Star and how to use weapons and equipment in the dark. We learned how to disperse in the surrounding woods in case of a night-time air attack, and how to hide from aircraft by day.

A couple of weeks after our arrival at Paplaka we received our first guns. The rifles were of French manufacture – short carbines, old and rusty. We had a lot of trouble cleaning and oiling these rifles, but they gave us a feel of being real soldiers. We marched with them hung on our shoulders and the face of our Company Commander shone with satisfaction at last on seeing us looking more military.

A few days before St John's Night[1] we received our first consignment of welfare goods, spirits and toilet requisites. The drinks were free and every man got one bottle, but we had to pay for the other things. I was on guard duty the following night and had a lot of trouble with drunken soldiers in order to keep them inside after the night-time roll call. It was late before everything became quiet. I had to keep walking around the barrack block to stop anyone from surprising the sleeping company. I had to be extra careful as I knew that officers from the neighbouring battalion used to approach the block in the night to test the alertness of the guards. I liked night duty. I could be my own master and nobody could interfere by giving me orders. Besides, I could sleep till dinner time the next day.

When I got up the Company was already preparing to leave for the Solemn Oath ceremony, after which we would be considered to be fully trained. Shortly before leaving our barracks I was handed a parcel from Bemberi with St John's Day cheese and other fine country food. I had a hurried taste of the parcel's contents, and then had to run to join the Company which was already lined up on the road and ready to leave.

We marched along the dusty road to the manor of Paplaka, and there lined up with other soldiers of the Regiment on a grassy square. The soldiers were arranged along three sides of this square; on the fourth side there was a speakers' platform, and on each side of this were pyramids of rifles and machine guns. The rows of Legionnaires were straightened out by the officers, the officer in charge commanded 'Attention!' and reported to the Regimental Commander who, after climbing onto the platform, read out the words of the Soldier's Oath and we all repeated after him: 'In the name of God, I solemnly swear in the fight against Bolshevism unlimited obedience to the Commander of the German Armed Forces, Adolf Hitler. As a brave soldier I shall always be ready to give my life, if necessary, to keep this promise true.'

After a short speech by the Regimental Commander, we started to march back to our barracks, but when we arrived there we were not allowed to disperse straight away. The Company Commander read out the names of those who had been promoted in rank for their soldierly behaviour and knowledge. My name was among these so, after only six weeks' service, I was promoted to 'Rottenführer' and could stitch two 'hooks' on my right sleeve. In reality, this was a mistake as the Latvian officers did not know the German Army regulations. All those promoted should have been given the rank of 'Sturmmann'. 'Rottenführer' was a rank reserved for those who had held the 'Sturmmann' rank for some time.

In the afternoon we began to prepare to celebrate St John's Night. First to leave were the singers who had been practising for a couple of weeks. Then, when it was getting dark, the rest of the Company marched out, going to the same square where we had already been that morning. In the official part of the celebrations we listened to the choir singing and watched the bonfires of the night. The dancing and drinking started later. Soldiers mixed with the civilians who had been asked to attend the celebrations. Dancers did not lack partners, drinkers had plenty of beer and spirits, and we celebrated this ancient Latvian feast until early morning. Next day quite a few of the Legionnaires missed the morning roll call, but nobody minded this. The only comment our commander made was: 'Paplaka has not seen such f**king and drinking in its time!' and he was surely right.

A couple of days later our French carbines were exchanged for German rifles and machine pistols. Everyone expected an early departure for the front. We were trained intensively with the new weapons every day. During the training with machine pistols our Company Commander tried to impress on us the wisdom of staying calm and trying to fire single shots. 'Aim directly into the foreheads of the Russians when they attack. Keep your head, do not get excited or frightened and do not waste ammunition by firing long bursts,' he used to say. Perhaps it was just a coincidence, but I heard later that the bullet that killed him had hit him directly in his forehead.

About a week after St John's Day the tallest men were selected from our own and other companies to serve with the Guards Company of the Latvian Legion. I was among these men, and so one day I packed my belongings, took leave of my friends and went to the station where I joined a group of similarly tall men. An officer met us at the station and was in charge of us during the train journey.

Most of the soldiers of the regiment were sent to the front soon after I left – only the officers remained at Paplaka to train new recruits. This was the 3rd Training and Auxiliary Regiment of the Latvian Legion, commanded by Colonel Kripens. The unit was renamed later the 32nd Armed SS (Latvian) Infantry Regiment of the 15th SS Volunteers' Division.

Notes
1 Midsummer's Night. In Latvia this is as important a celebration as Bonfire Night in England, and notorious for drunkenness and debauchery. (*LB*)

Chapter 4

With the Guards Company in Riga, July to October 1943

We left the station of Paplaka late in the evening, and a short time before starting on our journey were told that we were being sent to Riga. This information pleased me as I was already thinking of leave and the possibility of visiting my mother. We travelled all night and reached Riga early in the morning. After leaving the railway station we had a long ride in a tram car to a suburb of Riga where we were stationed in the barracks of 'Krustabaznica', near a large lake. It took us a while to find the Guards Company, only to discover that the men had already left for training. The duty men had been left in the Company's quarters, and were occupied sweeping the floors and polishing the furniture. Compared with Paplaka everything was much cleaner and tidier. The soldiers were dressed better and they all wore jackboots. I knew the duty NCO for that day – his mother lived in the same building where my mother rented her flat, and they were good friends.

Young Zade – that was his name – told me that they had very strict discipline here. Although stationed in Riga, we would seldom get any leave. The least violation of the Company's rules, or un-tidiness, was punished by denial of leave on Saturdays. A lot of time was spent in formation marching, singing while marching, and generally in the development of military bearing and behaviour.

At dinner time the Company returned from training and we, the new arrivals, were presented to the Company Commander. He had the rank of Second Lieutenant and his name was Juraids. The First Platoon of the Company was commanded by the second officer of the Company – Lieutenant Ancans. Both these officers were young, but their chests were already richly decorated with various medals of the German Army. They had spent some considerable time at the front in Russia, and both had distinguished themselves there. The commander of the Second Platoon was Sergeant Ritums, and the Third Platoon was commanded by Sub-Lieutenant Saulitis. After our inspection the Company Commander realized that, compared to his men, we were badly dressed, and ordered us to be taken to the stores in the afternoon to get new uniforms. In Paplaka the fit of our uniforms had been considered to be of secondary importance, but here a good fit was imperative. In the afternoon I had the opportunity to explore our new barracks and their surroundings.

We were stationed on the second floor of a large brick building and there were three such buildings in the barracks. The barrack blocks were arranged along three sides of a cobbled square and each of them could house a whole battalion of soldiers. The barracks had been built before the First World War, during the Russian Czar's reign in Latvia, and they showed a correspondingly ugly style in their design. Since then countless numbers of soldiers had stayed here leaving their mark. On a windowsill I could still see the year 1917 scratched by an unknown hand at that time. On the fourth side of the yard, towards Riga, there was the entrance gate and guard room. There was also a soldiers' welfare club where we could buy watery German beer. A lot of smaller buildings were scattered all around the barrack blocks. These had been stables and field-gun storage huts for the Artillery Regiment of the Latvian Army before the war, and for this reason the barracks were some-times called the Artillery Barracks. A high fence enclosed the camp, and beyond this fence were the sand dunes surrounding the large lake, pine forests and suburban houses.

The evening passed quickly in trying on our new uniforms, polishing our jackboots, arranging lockers and making beds for the night. It was soon time for the evening roll call held in the square, lights out and sleep.

Early in the morning we were lined up in the square and arranged according to height. I had been selected for the Instructors' Company at Paplaka on account of my height, but here I was just tall enough to get assigned to the Third Platoon.[1] The Platoon

Commander, Sub-Lieutenant Saulitis, was older than the officers of the Company and a sensible chap. He often gathered us around him during breaks in training and said, 'Although you may not like the constant marching practice and rifle drill, you must realize that it is all for your own good.' Slapping a handy rifle butt, he added for good measure, 'This is your bread and butter. The better and quicker you manage to master rifle drill, the longer you will be able to stop here, far from the front line with its dangers and discomforts.'

The commander of the Second Platoon, Ritums, was a man of quite different calibre. He was a career soldier, a creep of the highest order and did not consider the welfare of his men. His attitude once caused a near revolt of the Second Platoon. While the men were going to the lake for a swim, he gave an order for them to sing, but for some reason this did not go well, and the following order was to run. Five minutes later the order to march and sing was repeated, without any better performance from the men. This time the running lasted for a considerable period, after which Ritums asked the men which they liked best, running or singing. To his obvious surprise the reply was unanimous: 'To run!' It was pure spite which urged his men to give this answer and they had to run again. It is hard to tell how long this would have continued. The Company Commander soon intervened on account of the lack of time left for swimming.

The weeks passed one after another. Each morning was spent on intensive marching and rifle drill. We marched uncountable times from one end of the barracks to the other. If we did not march, we had to stand lined up on the same road practising rifle and foot drill for hours, or training to salute our officers. We also had combat training in the fields and forests around Riga, but the main part of our training programme was concerned with marching and rifle drill, as it was the intention of the Legion's High Command to train the Guards Company for representative purposes. To start with the constant rifle drill was hard to bear but we got used to it eventually and started other, more interesting training. We did some target shooting on the rifle range and often all went to the cinema together. The Company would then march singing through the streets of Riga to show the people the proud bearing of their own soldiers.

The most popular duty was guarding the Headquarters of the Latvian Legion, which was situated in Pardaugava on the other side of the river, and not far from my mother's flat. A German corporal was usually in charge of the six-man guard. After arrival at the Headquarters we were inspected by a German officer who was responsible for security and general duties within the Latvian Legion. The inspection was very strict and the officer would shout angrily if anyone's boots were not sufficiently shiny or anything else was not in order. After the inspection we took over from the sentries of the previous guard. Four men and the NCO stayed in the guard room, a sentry was mounted on the gate and one man sat at a table in the entrance hall of the Headquarters. The gate guard had to salute each arriving officer, and we were able to make good use of our training and rifle drill. A sloppy salute resulted in a report by the officer to our NCO, and the offending man could be sure of extra drill when returning to barracks. The man in the entrance hall informed officers arriving of the whereabouts of the various departments of the Legion. Whenever I had to go on guard duty at the Headquarters, I telephoned my mother. She could visit me there during off-duty hours, and usually brought specially nice food which she had prepared for me.

In the evening, when work at the Headquarters ended, the guards were left in sole charge of the building. When it started to get dark we checked all the windows to make sure they were tightly shut. The kitchens were in the cellars and we often found an open window. We would then climb in and feed ourselves on all sorts of fancy dishes left over from the officers' meals. To avoid suspicion we always managed to capture a cat during the night and let it loose in the kitchen. At night one guard stood at the gate, while two others patrolled the grounds. It was very monotonous to stand still near the gate and the guard often fell asleep. On one occasion one of the gate sentries had actually left his post and had gone for a sleep in one of the cars parked in the grounds. He awoke only as the car was being driven through the gates by an officer's driver. Luckily we managed to keep this event a secret otherwise the man would have had to face a court martial.

Representing the Legion, we once took part in a senior officer's funeral at which we were supposed to fire our rifles in unison as a final tribute. We were unable to achieve this because there was insufficient time to practise for the occasion, and our shooting sounded more like rifle fire on a battlefield. It was not really our fault and yet, next day, we had an extra rifle drill as punishment for our poor performance.

On 23 September 1943 the Commander of the SS, Himmler, visited Riga for a conference with local SS commanders. That day we were told to get our equipment and weapons in especially good order. Around dinner time we all got into lorries and were driven to Riga airport to receive Himmler. We had to mount a guard of honour at the airport and, after lining up, we had to wait about an hour before the VIP arrived. The aircraft circled the field a couple of times, landed and taxied to a stop opposite us. We stood to attention while our Company Commander reported to our supreme commander. Himmler walked slowly past the Company examining each man with his small piercing eyes, hidden behind the glass of his spectacles. He then got into a car and was driven away towards Riga. We boarded our lorries for the drive back to the barracks, but the Company Commander had different ideas. We had to dismount near the main railway station of Riga and march through the streets followed by a large crowd of people. Men, women and children kept pace with us during the march and from their faces we could see that they were proud of their Legionnaires.

A couple of days later we got the order for quite a different kind of guard duty. We had to guard Latvians who had deserted from the Red Army, and were temporarily stationed in a school while awaiting the order to be demobilized. Their previous guards, somewhere in Poland or Germany, had been German SS and had terrified the Latvians with their inhuman treatment of them. Even now, while guarding them, the prisoners respectfully stepped aside when we walked through the barrack rooms. We found out that the Germans had beaten and kicked them every time that they had been in their way. The Latvians had had a very difficult time with the Red Army. The food had been poor, they had strict discipline maintained by political commissars and had lived in primitive conditions all the time. These prisoners longed for the day when their fate would be decided and, they hoped, they would be able to join in the fight against the Bolshevists, or return to normal life as civilians.

This was my last guard duty while with the Guards Company. In late September I and others were ordered to Bolderaja as instructors in the newly formed Signals Unit of the Legion.

Notes
1 My father was 6 feet tall. (*LB*)

Chapter 5

Instructor with a Signals Unit, Bolderaja, October 1943

Bolderaja was a small fishing village, a suburb of Riga, about 5 miles north of the town. The eastern and northern boundaries of the village were formed by the river Daugava and as the sea was only a couple of miles away, one could always hear the sound of the waves beating the shore. There were only a few streets of small, weatherbeaten and dilapidated houses. The surrounding country-side consisted of extensive pine forests.

The largest building was the school, a brick building four storeys high and a late addition to the village. We had been told to report there for duty with the Signals Unit. When we entered the school we found it empty and quiet, and had to search for some time before we found the office and the officer commanding the Signals Unit. The Lieutenant was surprised by our arrival and told us that he had not expected any instructors so soon. As there was nothing for us to do, the officer had no objection to our returning to Riga until the following morning. He wrote out the necessary passes and allowed us to go, provided that we returned early the next day, by which time he would have something for us to do. An hour after our arrival in Bolderaja we all boarded the bus and returned to Riga.

During the next month with the Signals unit we instructors got plenty of leave and I spent many days at home. The new recruits were in a different position, however, and did not get any leave at all during the first three weeks of their service. Even later, a hopeful

31

leave taker often had to stay at the school following a pre-leave inspection. The Sergeant Major was very strict in this respect and did not allow any disorder in the recruits' uniforms or equipment. The new lads had nothing to do at the school in the evenings and had to lie on their beds listening to the autumn wind whistling around corners in the dark night outside.

When we reported back the next morning we were told to put the rooms in order and assemble some wooden bunk beds; we also had the job of filling mattresses with wood shavings. After we had got a good supply of bed ends, sides and boards into a top-storey room and had started to put the beds together, we discovered that they were full of bugs. We did not think much of this, but the officer ordered us to carry the beds down into the yard and exchange them for new ones. After a few trips down the stairs we found a new, more acceptable way of getting the beds into the yard – we simply pushed the ends and sides out through the windows, from where they fell straight down into the school yard. The job was soon done and the only casualty was a first-storey window, shattered by a board falling from a top window. The Company Commander became angry about this, but in the evening, seeing that we had got all the rooms in order, he let us have our leave passes. We spent another couple of days tidying up the school rooms, by which time the new recruits were beginning to arrive to start their service with the Legion.

These new recruits were mostly young lads, schoolboys, country youths and young workers. Until then they had led a sheltered, easy life, pampered and looked after by their mothers – understandably they had great difficulty in adapting to life in the Army. They had to look after their arms and equipment, and had to keep their uniforms clean and their boots polished; they had to train with signals equipment and learn to march and sing; they had to comply with orders to the letter and learn discipline the hard way. Every violation of the rules resulted in some form of punishment. They had to get up early and go outside for morning exercises, followed by a mile-long run to the river to wash in cold water. At dinner time a couple of recruits had to serve meals to the officers and instructors in their rooms, and keep the Company's quarters clean and tidy. There were a few cases of desertion by recruits who could not stand this period of harsh discipline. Deserters never returned to Bolderaja, but if they had been captured their names were displayed

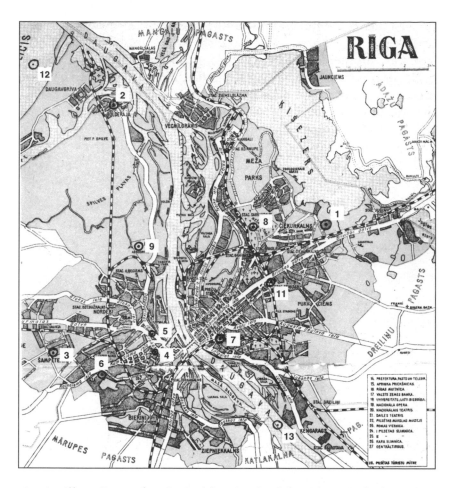

1. Artillery Barracks. 2. Bolderaja. 3. Schampeteris fuel Depot.
4. My Mother's Flat. 5. Latvian Legion Headquarters.
6. Ventspils Street. 7. Riga Railway Station. 8. War Cemetery.
9. Riga Airport. 10. Vecaki and Rinuzi Stations.
11. St Zemitani. 12. The Bay of Riga. 13. River Daugava.

on the notice board. Exercises with telephone and radio equipment
were held in the forests and fields around the village. Marching and
rifle drill were carried out on sandy tracks with us, the instructors,
commanding the whole Company. During signals training we were
free and could do whatever we liked.

All October passed in training and exercises, but towards the end of the month we were told that the unit would be moved to Tukums, another seaside town but much further from Riga. Some of the instructors went with the Signals Unit, but I and others were ordered to return to the Guards Company in Riga. On arrival at the Artillery Barracks we saw a lot of new faces. Most of the men who had served with the Guards during the summer had been posted to different regiments of the Legion as instructors. The officers and instructors of the Company were still in Riga and were already training a new consignment of recruits. The next day I and about a platoon of ex-guardsmen, were sent once more to Paplaka to instruct a new regiment of men.

Chapter 6

Instructor at Paplaka,
November 1943

In the spring, when I first arrived at Paplaka, the weather was mostly sunny, the trees were sprouting new leaves and we were in the best of spirits. Now, in the autumn, on the way from the station to the barracks, we had to struggle through roadside mud and a fine rain fell from the lead-grey sky.

It was already dark when we reached the barracks. Unlike our last place of service, we were expected here. The new recruits had already been in Paplaka for a couple of days. As the lack of instructors had delayed the establishment of proper discipline and weapon training we were straight away assigned to the various companies and sent to report to our new commanders. I was given the post of a section commander with the First Company of the Regiment, which was quartered in the same building where I had spent my first night with the Legion in the spring. Other ex-guardsmen were assigned to better duties. During my service at Bolderaja they had remained with the Guards Company in Riga and had all been promoted to the rank of corporal. Here they were given the command of platoons, while some were even made Company Sergeant Majors and had their own separate rooms. I had to sleep and live with the recruits in the large common room. It was dark there in the evenings, the only illumination provided by a few electric bulbs. As electricity was in short supply, the light bulbs often only glowed faintly in the dark room. There was not much heating and the winds of late autumn could easily get in around the badly fitting window frames.

The new recruits consisted of older men who had so far managed to escape being called up, and young lads who would rather have been looked after by their mothers. They were all in poor spirits and there was no discipline. These new Legionnaires were quite different in character to those who started service with the spring call-up. Whereas we were all full of the spirit of adventure, the new draft seemed to be serving against their own free will. There was even one man in my company who seemed to be mentally unfit to serve in the Armed Forces. He had once served with the French Foreign Legion and often used to tell horrifying tales about his experiences there.

I had no common interests with these men in my free time, and other instructors felt the same way. We spent our evenings together in the Company Sergeant Major's room. He often had the opportunity to obtain extras to eat and drink, and gladly shared his spoils with his comrades from the Guards Company. We played cards, listened to the wireless or occupied ourselves otherwise until late into the night. If there was nothing else to do in the evenings, the Sergeant Major sometimes tested the Company's readiness for action. He would order the whole Company to parade in the yard in full battle order, the time set for this being five minutes. Those who arrived in the yard after the time limit were separated from the others. After the rest of the Company had returned to their quarters, the defaulters had extra drill in the corridors, and this continued until the men were completely exhausted. We, the instructors, had to give the necessary commands and orders, and thus remain up until late in the night, but we did not mind. We wanted the recruits to get a taste of the same disciplinary punishments which we ourselves had suffered while they had been living in peace.

At first, the Company Commander, Captain Lidums, did not like our separation from the recruits and our gatherings in the Sergeant Major's room. He did not even like our strict handling of the recruits, but after a few days he began to realize that our disciplinary methods were right. We knew the various regulations of the German Army much better than any of the officers. Most of them had been commissioned in the Latvian Army and were not familiar with the present methods of training. We had a case where an officer was explaining one way of handling a machine gun, while the instructors were demonstrating another way of doing the same thing. Afterwards, all instructors were ordered to report to the

Company Office where the Company Commander began by shouting angrily about our disrespect for the officers and lack of knowledge. To explain his reasons for disagreement with the officer's method, one of the instructors concerned had to show the Book of Regulations to the Company Commander. After this incident Captain Lidums did not try to improve our methods of teaching, nor did he attempt to stop our get-togethers in the Sergeant Major's room as he could see that the discipline and general behaviour of his soldiers was improving day by day.

Within a couple of weeks the new men and boys of the Company became proper soldiers, thanks to our strict discipline. Everyone felt that we would not stay in Paplaka for long and would soon leave for the front. With the approach of 18 November, Latvian Independence Day, a new rumour began to circulate among the men: as a reward for the Latvians' help in the battle against the Bolshevists, the Germans were supposed to be ready to recognize Latvia as a free state. Unfortunately these rumours proved to be without foundation. On the morning of 18 November the Regiment assembled on the same square where that spring we had given the Solemn Soldier's Oath. The Regimental Commander, Kripens, spoke to us about the meaning of this day to all Latvians, and our duty in helping the German Army to prevent a second occupation of Latvia by the Red Army. He did not, however, mention anything about independence and after a march past we quietly dispersed to our quarters.

That afternoon there was no rifle drill or training. We were going to celebrate, and to do so we went to the Mess and sat down at long tables for our special dinner. A small portion of our rations had been saved for a couple of days for the occasion and each man had a full bottle of strong drink in front of him. Before the dinner our Company Commander had a few words to say to his men. He started by explaining that his and the instructors' strict handling of the new recruits until now had been for their own good. It was highly probable that very soon we would have to depart for the front, where a soldier without discipline was no good to anyone and was even a danger to himself. The CO finished his speech with the words: 'Let's drink and be merry, then, while we can, and when we reach the front line, let's fight like men who are not afraid of the Devil himself.'

The bottles were soon half empty, singing and talking became louder, and very soon a couple of new recruits had forgotten their respect for the officer so much so that they were offering him drinks straight from the bottle. When all the bottles were empty the men started to leave the Mess room and go to their own quarters to sleep or to continue drinking from their supplies of 'moonshine'.

The Company Commander called me over straight after we had left the Mess. Speaking with difficulty he managed to slap me on the shoulder and said, 'You're one of the more educated of my men, so next week I'm sending you to Riga for a course on gas warfare.' After this short announcement he staggered away towards his room supported by the Sergeant Major.

Battle training continued all the following week. Because of the anticipated departure for the front, we paid most attention to weapon training, even managing to carry out a night march and training in the field to introduce the new soldiers to battlefield conditions.

The battle exercises and weapon training ceased altogether by the end of November, and the Regiment started to prepare to leave Paplaka. We heard rumours of an attempt to poison a whole battalion of soldiers of our neighbouring regiment, the 33rd Regiment of the Latvian Legion stationed at Vainode. Poison had been added to a meal prepared for the Battalion in a common field kitchen. Our men were very upset about this and expressed the view that the guilty man should be shot without trial. The guilty person, a Communist agent and himself serving with the neighbouring Regiment, was caught and executed.

Meanwhile, we were issued with the long-awaited heavy weapons. Our Company had to go to the Forest Camp and carry the heavy legs and barrels of the 8cm mortars, new machine guns, wireless equipment and heavy boxes of ammunition. Horses pulled the field kitchen and carts loaded with mortar ammunition and hand grenades. There was a lot of activity everywhere to prepare for the journey to the station.

I and the other men who had been assigned to take part in the Chemical Warfare course in Riga did not have to participate in the various activities in connection with the loading of equipment. Instead, I packed my rucksack, said goodbye to my friends and went to the Forest Camp where we had been told to report. From there, led by Lieutenant Berzins, we left for the railway station, walking straight across fields through the sticky mud. The going was heavy and the horses of the Regiment's transport did not fare any better in pulling the loaded carts along the waterlogged roads towards the station.

Soldiers of the Regiment had taken over the station almost completely and were busy loading equipment onto railway wagons. Loud curses filled the air, while officers were engaged in checking the correct sequence of loading and the coupling of wagons to the train. The Regiment was supposed to leave in the morning – there was not much time to lose. I heard later that the men of my Company had made their own battle flag and attached it to the Company Commander's compartment. They had painted a skull and crossbones on the flag, followed by an inscription 'TO SMASH, F**K AND DESTROY'. Their spirits had been high.

We awaited the arrival of our train and started on our way to Riga and the Chemical Warfare course. Our first stop was Liepaja where we had to wait for the train to Riga. It was dark and wet outside. A drizzle of rain mixed with fog descended on the town, and I spent all the waiting time in the station soldiers' club reading newspapers and magazines. It was completely dark when the train finally arrived and we travelled all night, reaching Riga around 8 o'clock in the morning. By then the sun had broken through the grey rain clouds and shone brightly over the city.

Chapter 7

Chemical Warfare Course, Riga, December 1943

Led by Lieutenant Berzins, we went from one military office to another trying to find out where we were supposed to report. We could not obtain any clear information regarding this matter, and in the end the Lieutenant did not know what to do. He assembled us all around him and asked whether we would be able to stay in Riga on our own for a couple of days. The answer was obvious: everyone could manage this quite easily. The officer made us promise him to report back and then allowed us to go on leave on our word of honour. We arranged to meet in the centre of the town in the morning at 10.00 a.m., but before dispersing the officer gave each of us his address, and told us to get in touch with him if we were detained by the Military Police. I had hoped for some leave since arriving in Riga; now I caught the first tram and was on my way home. First I had to go to my mother's place of work to obtain the key for the flat – only then could I go home. I walked through the streets keeping a careful watch for any Military Police and reached the flat without difficulty.

That evening I had a bath and went to bed between clean sheets. Having slept most of the previous night on the train I was not tired and spent most of the night reading my old books.

The next day we met as arranged, but stayed together for only a short time. Our Lieutenant still knew nothing more concerning the arrangements for our course. Perhaps he had not tried too hard to obtain the necessary information as he himself would want to use this opportunity to spend some time away from the Army. We arranged to meet again in a couple of days and each of us went his own way.

A couple of days later, when we met again in the centre of town, Lieutenant Berzins announced that he had found out where we were to report for the gas course. First we had to get onto a tram and ride to his flat. There the officer took leave of his wife or mistress, and we began the march to the barracks quite near to the main railway station of Riga. We were shown two rooms that had been allocated for the course. They were dirty and the floors were covered by a thick layer of dirt and papers. A Dutch unit had been stationed there before us – in the two rooms we found a lot of their newspapers and peculiar clogs. Our group was the first to arrive from various regiments for the course, and therefore had the job of cleaning out our quarters. For a couple of days we had plenty to do. We swept out the dirt, clogs, newspapers, empty tins and pieces of Dutch cheese, and after that we washed the floors. The only thing we found of any value here were bags of good Dutch coffee – much better than the stuff issued by the German Army. I gathered a lot of packets of coffee and took them home to my mother. She was glad to have it. At that time good coffee cost a lot of money – when it was obtainable on the black market. When the rooms were clean we could begin to live in them. A few days later groups of men from other regiments started to arrive and the course could begin.

At first the lectures were held inside. We got to know the characteristics of gases used in warfare and the preventative measures against them. We learned the fitting and use of gas masks. During a realistic demonstration we had to enter a gas-filled room with the mask on, remove the mask and once more put it on. We had to hold our breath while doing this, of course, but some men forgot and came out spluttering with tears running down their faces. We later tried out the preventative measures in the fields surrounding the town, and among the allotments of suburban Riga. We fenced off and marked a region which was supposed to be poisoned by gas, dressed in the protective clothing and entered the field to make it safe. We marched with gas masks on and even had to sing, or rather shout so that the officers could hear the song at all.

During the couple of weeks spent at the course we acquired little more than a superficial knowledge about chemical warfare. I do not think our knowledge would have been of any use if gas had ever been used in the war. It is possible that the intention was to prepare chemical warfare specialists for the regiments of the Legion, but we were never assigned to any such duties. Every soldier at the front was supplied with a gas mask. Most of them, however, did not carry their masks with them and used the round containers for other purposes. Many men stuffed the containers with food and cigarettes, or even using them as cooking utensils. Luckily, gas was not used during the war, otherwise the results would have been terrible.

On 23 December I and a group of men were ordered to guard an ammunitions train. We climbed onto lorries and drove to Vecaki, a small suburb about 8 miles north of Riga. There, in the middle of the pine forest, were concrete bunkers which had been used for ammunition storage when Latvia was independent. When retreating from Latvia in 1941, the Russians had tried to blow up the bunkers, but they had been repaired and used once more for the same purpose. As the railway line did not reach the bunkers we had to carry and load field gun ammunition and charges onto lorries. After a short drive to the railway station of Rinuzi, we had to unload the ammunition from the lorries onto railway wagons. When loading was completed we were shown an empty wagon as our quarters, from where we had to guard the train. We had an oven and as we could get coal from the locomotive, we did not have to worry about the cold. Two of us were stationed each side of the train while it was stationary, against any possible attempt by Bolshevist agents to blow up the ammunition. The rest stayed in the wagon and spent a lot of time discussing the possibility of Christmas leave.

After some hours at Rinuzi the train was moved to a branch line near the Artillery Barracks, arriving there late at night and remaining there all the next day. That evening the train was moved to Zemitani station, quite near the centre of the town, and we were told that we would stay there all night.

It was Christmas Eve and there was no hope of getting any leave. One of the guards, Pommers, decided to chance his luck and get home for a few hours. He lived near to my mother's flat and I asked him to visit her as well. I gave Pommers a short note for my mother in which I explained why I was not able to get home for Christmas Eve, and asked her to send me some holiday fare. Pommers got out of the station without much difficulty and rode off in a tram towards the town centre.

It began to snow steadily and soon everything was covered with fresh white snow. One of us obtained a Christmas tree from somewhere and we also managed to provide a few candles. All around us in the town the celebrations were going in full swing. Some of the men left the station and returned with bottles in their pockets, bringing with them a couple of semi-drunk girls. Pommers also returned bringing with him some buns from his mother and mine as well, so now we could start our Christmas celebrations in the wagon.

Nobody guarded the train any more. There was not much point in doing so. We did not believe there would be an attempt to blow up the train in the middle of the town. We lit the candles on the tree, sang the usual carols, ate and drank. The girls put our caps on their heads and our belts around their waists. Dressed this way they marched along the platform of the station and nobody took any notice of them. We had decided to celebrate Christmas and did not care about tomorrow. When the first lot of bottles were empty, somebody went into town and returned with another load of full bottles and the party continued.

It was the early hours of the morning. Most of us were sleeping off the effects of the drink when suddenly there were shouts from outside for the guard. It was a German voice and soon someone was beating a tattoo on the closed wagon doors. We were on our feet in a moment, opened the door on the other side of the train and pushed the girls out. One of us grabbed a rifle and jumped out with them pretending to be on guard. Then, after tidying up a little, we opened the door which was being hammered on by a German officer. His first question was for the guard, and luckily the guard answered the officer from the other side of the train. On seeing him the officer quietened down. He said a few words about drinking while on duty and then told us that our services were not needed any more. Soon afterwards a fresh locomotive was attached to the train and it began to move away towards its destination – the front in Russia. We were left behind with aching heads, boarded a tram and returned to the barracks.

I was free all Christmas Day, free from any duty at the barracks having been guarding the train. I slept all day and in the evening went on leave. My mother kept saying how sorry she was for me not to be able to spend Christmas Eve at home. Little did she know how I had spent the last night!

Back at the barracks the Chemical Warfare course had ended and a couple of days later I was ordered to accompany the driver of an army lorry on the way to Jelgava. We left Riga in the afternoon of 27 December, reached Jelgava in the late evening and were told to stay the night at the High School of Duke Peter. We had our breakfast there the next morning and soon left for the goods yard of Jelgava station where we had to load field-gun carriages onto the lorries of the Artillery Division of the Latvian Legion. The Division and its guns were already in Russia. We had to transport the gun carriages to Majevo station in Russia and there our duties would end. From Majevo we would be sent back to our own units of the Legion. My life behind the front line had ended. I could not complain – most of my friends had already been in Russia for some time.

We left for Riga in the afternoon and arrived at our barracks as it was already getting dark. We had to leave again a short time later, this time to the manor of Schampeteris, a few miles outside Riga, to fill the fuel tanks of our lorries to capacity for the long drive ahead. The Schampeteris fuel depot was situated in the middle of a forest and was the main fuel depot for all the region of Riga. We had to wait a long time in a queue for our petrol. This scarce commodity was treated like water there, with the soil in the forest soaked in fuel. We saw large puddles of it at the roadsides and the very air was filled with the reek of petrol and oil. The Germans filling our tanks took no notice of this, smoking cigarettes while handling the fuel pipes and pumping the petrol straight from the metal barrels, and throwing lighted matches and cigarette ends on the ground. They behaved exactly as if they were handling water. I expected the forest to explode like a bomb at any moment and was glad to get out of there.

Part II

The Russian Front

Chapter 8

The Drive to Russia and the Front Line, January 1944

It was a cold sunny morning on 29 December when we left Riga, driving along the highway of Vidzeme towards the north in a convoy of about fifteen heavy lorries. Each driver had one of us with him as a guard and mate on the long drive. In the beginning the highway was slippery, covered with a thin layer of ice and we had to proceed carefully. When we had left the suburbs of Riga behind us parts of the road were covered with snow. All around us were snow-covered fields and pine forests. Only occasionally did we see a farm encircled by snowy plains and hillocks, the only sign of life being the thin smoke rising from the chimney.

We reached Sigulda around dinner time and stopped for a short rest. It was cold in the driver's cabin while the engine was not running, so I left the lorry and went into a nearby shop. I could spend my last food coupons there and get warm. I spent an hour there talking with civilian shoppers most of whom were country folk from the surrounding farms. When the men got to know that we were on our way to Russia, they produced bottles of strong drink from their pockets. Once more we had to drink a few glasses of vodka to ensure our good luck for the future.

We were on the road all afternoon, driving through the district of Vidzeme. When it got dark we continued our drive through the hilly country of northern Latvia by the light of dimmed head-lamps. It became very cold and even with the engine running I could feel my toes stiffening. At about 9.00 p.m. we turned off the highway and continued the drive up a small country road.

Half an hour later we arrived in the yard of a large building and were told we would spend the night there. A sign over the door announced that this was 'THE PRIMARY SCHOOL OF TRAPENE' and now we knew that we were near the northern border of Latvia. One of the classrooms was already prepared for us. There were beds with straw-filled mattresses but no blankets. This did not worry us in the least as each soldier had a couple of blankets with him from Riga – and besides, it was warm enough inside. A large stove spread welcoming warmth around it, and after a simple supper we all went to sleep warm and contented.

On the morning of 30 December we had a pleasant surprise. As soon as we got up we were invited to breakfast in the school hall where tables were already set with a good meal. We were served by women of the local Home Guard and discovered that they had got to know about our arrival only late the previous evening. The women had toured the surrounding farms collecting donations of food, and afterwards spent the whole night baking and cooking to prepare our breakfast of fresh bread, meat pies and jam tarts. We sincerely thanked the leader of the Home Guard for their kindness and effort, but she replied that everything had been done voluntarily, adding that it was the least that they could do to show their thanks to the Latvian soldiers in their fight against the Bolsheviks. There was a lot of food left over when we had finished our breakfast and this was distributed among us. We filled our water bottles with milk and then it was time to leave the kind people of Trapene.

We were soon back on the highway as it neared the border of Estonia. The driving was much slower than on the day before as it had been snowing during the night. In many places there were snowdrifts right across the road. The country around us was hilly and covered with extensive pine forests. One of the lorries broke down and we all had to stop and wait until it was repaired so that in the evening the distance covered was much shorter than that of the previous day. We stopped for the night at Izborsk, a village near the border between Estonia and Russia.

The previous night there was nothing to indicate that there was a war going on, but here one could feel the proximity of the front line. There were a great many soldiers about and army vehicles were driving to and fro. We parked our lorries in a large square, the forecourt of an inn. Although I had become cold during the latter part of our drive, I still had to stand guard by our lorries for a couple of hours before I could go into our sleeping quarters. While climbing the stairs to the second storey of the inn I had a sudden fright – an enormous stuffed brown bear, very lifelike, stood on its back legs in a stair corner. This bear, with his lifeless glassy eyes, regarded me and the other sleepers all night while we slept on the straw-covered floor of the dark room. This room was filled to capacity with soldiers, so I had to search for some time before I could find a space large enough to lie down.

When we continued our drive the next morning I noticed that I had acquired the property of a front-line soldier – lice. I could not do anything about this other than scratch and bear with the unwanted inhabitants of my clothes. Quite soon we crossed the Russian frontier and continued to drive along a highway running parallel with the eastern border of Latvia and Russia. We reached Ostrova around dinner time, had a short rest there and carried on driving. It was easy going here. The highway was free from snow which had been pushed aside by snow ploughs, forming high banks on both sides of the road. The country was flat and empty, with only occasional trees and houses. The road was constantly guarded from partisans by German soldiers stationed at frequent intervals in fortified strongpoints, and fighter aircraft often patrolled the air above to protect the convoys heading for the front from air attacks. We made good progress and reached Opochka in the evening. This was a largish town and we were to spend the night here.

Just in front of the barracks there was a large square full of people trading in various things. Russian civilians mixed freely with German soldiers and uniformed German women – members of the German Signals units – employed as telephone operators and clerks. The Germans were preparing to celebrate the New Year and were buying or exchanging chickens, eggs, smoked bacon, onions and lard. There was a lot of noise and shouting, bottles of drink were to be seen in hands and pockets, and everybody was in a cheerful mood – except for me. While freezing in the driver's cab I had caught a cold, my head was aching and I had a temperature. I had saved a lot of cigarettes and used forty of these to bribe one of my mates to take over my period of guard duty outside. Having settled this I took some aspirins and went to sleep.

I was awakened in the middle of the night by a great noise outside. The New Year had just arrived and many shots were fired to greet 1944. Hand grenades exploded all around the barracks and there was a lot of shouting while all the windows blazed with the lights of rockets. A short time later the door to the sleeping quarters was wrenched open and a crowd of drunken Germans rushed in. They wanted to wish a Happy New Year to those sleeping and produced bottles from their pockets from which we had to drink as was the practice on such occasions. The drinking continued for about an hour and only then were we able to go back to sleep.

I got up late the next morning, 1 January 1944. Many of the men were still half drunk, the rest had headaches and hangovers, and so we were unable to continue our journey until midday. Driving along the highway we soon reached Pustochka from where we turned off onto a smaller road leading directly east – towards the front line. Pustochka was an important road junction. Through this village passed all military transports for the front-line sector opposite Nowo Sokolniki and Velikai Luki. When we arrived in the village a traffic jam was just being sorted out. The road was filled with lorries, tracked vehicles, tanks and motorcycles and the Military Police were busy trying to disentangle this jam. Slowly, but without too much delay, the long line of vehicles moved forward, through Pustochka, past the grey wooden houses and out into the country. Behind the village many roads branched off the main one, the driving was easier and we progressed quickly. The weather became warmer, the snow began to melt and very soon we had to drive carefully once more. Now and then the wheels began to slip without gripping the road as we went uphill. We had to get out of the driver's cabin, call for help to push and supplement the power of the engine, and thus reach the top of the hill.

In the evening it began to snow. The snow-covered road slowed our progress still more, and so it was late at night that we arrived at our destination – the station of Majevo. We drove into the station yard and had to spend the night there. Night quarters for soldiers were quite near the station, but they were already filled to capacity. Soldiers slept on the floor right up to the door and we could not get in. Each of us received a couple of pints of hot soup from the cookhouse for our supper before returning to our lorries. We had to spend the freezing night in the drivers' cabs. We lit a small paraffin heater which was otherwise used to keep the engine from freezing, but this did not give much warmth. It became so cold during the night that we could not sleep and often had to jump out of the cabin, run around the lorry and warm our stiffening toes. Feeling miserable and half asleep we greeted the sunny morning of 2 January 1944.

The station of Majevo was a main supply point for the front line of this sector. As a result of the recent Russian attack on Novo Sokolniki and Nevel, the station was full of supply trains and troops; there was activity everywhere. Trains arrived and were quickly unloaded onto lorries for onward transport to the front. Empty trains left in the direction of Pskov followed by several trains of wounded soldiers going in the same direction, slowly passing other trains loaded with reinforcements.

I and other men of the 32nd Regiment of the Legion were driven in lorries to Regimental Headquarters in a Russian village. We arrived there around dinner time and after being assigned to our units, were shown the way to the surrounding villages where they were stationed. When I arrived at the supply depot of the 1st Company I was received with open arms. The Sergeant Major told me that life here was quite good. They lived in a wooden house, it was possible to trade or steal a few sheep from Russian civilians to supplement the rations, and they had even managed to organize the brewing of home-made beer. They had plenty of fuel for the stove from an empty house nearby which the soldiers were gradually pulling down, and burning the wood. The only complaint the Sergeant Major had was about the local Russian women, most of whom were old. He had tried to get one of the younger ones to sleep with him the previous night, but she would not hear of it. The woman had even threatened him with notifying the partisans about his behaviour and this had been the main reason why he had let her go. He did not wish to make enemies of the partisans because until now they had let us live in peace. All the men from the Company had been assigned to German units in the front line, about 15 miles away. I was told I would be going there the next day with a group of men who had been left behind for some reason, or had arrived later than the main body of the Company. Our Company Commander was already there and I was to report to him when we arrived. The Sergeant Major appointed me leader of the group because of my rank and knowledge of the German language.

It was freezing outside that night. We kept the stove going full blast, and yet the windows behind the sills covered with hand grenades soon became covered with frost. Outside one could see the faint lights of front-line rockets, and somewhere towards Majevo the sound of an aircraft hung in the air, which was criss-crossed by tracer, but everything was quiet in our village. The only people awake were the stove minder and a guard outside. Even the man watching the stove was armed with a machine pistol to defend the house from possible partisan attack, and to allow time for the others to get up and grab their weapons.

We got up early in the morning, had our breakfast while it was still dark, and then set off on our route march to the front line. After a short distance we reached a river and crossed it by going carefully over the ice. We knew that a couple of days before the ice had broken while a supply sledge was crossing, and the driver and horse had only just escaped from drowning. On reaching the other side we continued to march straight across the fields. I used a map and compass to find the shortest route to the front line and we came to the main road just as the sun was rising. While passing through a village we smelled the aroma of freshly baked bread. The Bakery Company of our Division was stationed here and after a short bargaining session each of us received a fresh loaf from the bakers in exchange for a few cigarettes.

Soon after we had left the village behind us, the road started to climb a range of hills from the top of which we had a good view towards the east. We had not noticed any signs of war until now, but the plain on the other side of the hills told a different story. All the houses of the villages had either been pulled down or burnt to the ground – only the brick chimneys remained standing to indicate the places where the homes of Russian peasants had once stood. Over the wide plain we could see another row of low hills on the eastern horizon. Long poles had been put up at frequent intervals on both sides of the road ahead of us.

Each pair of poles was connected across the road with wire from which hung long cloth ribbons and bundles of straw. This was a kind of camouflage, intended to stop the Russian observers from seeing any traffic passing along the road and directing their artillery fire.

Continuing across the plain we made for the remains of a village situated on a low mound surrounded by a few trees. Just after we had left the ruins behind us, a German suddenly emerged from a well-hidden dugout and called us back. He told us that we would be mad to march openly along the road as Russian artillery fired on anything moving there and advised us to go back a little way and take another road.

From the heights of this village we obtained our first glimpse of the front line. We could hear the distant rumble of field guns and see the explosions of shells which were throwing up lofty fountains of snow that glittered in the sun on the horizon. We thanked the German for the warning and went on our way following his directions.

After passing several ruined villages in the late afternoon we reached the range of hills we had seen that morning. We could now distinctly feel the nearness of the front line and could clearly hear the sound of artillery, while high above us an air battle was in progress – German fighter planes were attacking a Russian aircraft formation. We crossed a small river by a wooden bridge and the road began to climb a high bank on the other side. To obtain further directions I visited a German bunker by the road-side and then we continued on our way. After crossing the range of hills along the eastern bank of the river the road led directly to the front line and we could not get lost now. According to the map we had to march another 3 miles.

It became dark and a fresh snowstorm started as we marched. In front of us we could hear rifle and machine-gun fire which, in the snow-filled air, had lost all its crispness and sounded soft and quite friendly.

A short while later we saw on the left-hand side of the road a simple signpost inscribed 'BUNKERTOWN BOJAKI' – the place I had been told to find in the morning – and knew that our long walk was near its end. Following a snow-covered path we soon reached a hillside with several bunkers dug into it. This was the Headquarters of the German unit to which we had been assigned.

I went into one of the bunkers, reported our arrival to a German officer and had to wait while he telephoned the various front-line sub-units to which we were to be sent. He also telephoned a neighbouring bunker to inform our Company Commander. Captain Lidums came straight away, greeted us and told us that we were lucky to be there. According to him, this was a quiet sector of the front line and relations with the Germans were good.

The Headquarters bunkers were truly magnificent. Each of them had a large fireplace, wooden tables and benches, and the walls were hung with embroidered soldiers' blankets. The wooden floorboards were scrubbed white. A decorated Christmas tree still stood in one corner on a small cupboard with glass doors through which I could see a number of bottles – a cocktail cabinet, no doubt.

Half an hour later our guides arrived from the front line. We left the Headquarters, split up and each went his way following the Germans through the snowstorm just behind the forward trenches. Now and then we heard a few shots and saw a rocket ascend which soon lost its brilliance in the snow-filled air. We reached the front-line trenches and, walking along them, soon came to the bunker which was to be my home. We climbed down steep stairs, opened a squeaky door and entered the underground cavern.

It was dark in the bunker. The only light came from the open door of a cast-iron stove. Six Germans sat around the stove waiting for their dinners to warm up. They had hung their mess tins on hooks all around the red-hot stove which was the focal point of the bunker. After the usual introductions I opened my rucksack, took out a candle and lit it to the great delight of my new comrades. Candles were scarce at the front line and they had long since used up their monthly ration. By day the Russian artillery prevented any supplies reaching the trenches: this explained why they were reheating their food which they received in the late evening when Russian observers could not see the approach of the supply columns. The Germans offered me some of their own food, but I refused it. I was so tired after the all-day march that I could not keep awake. After drinking a mug of hot coffee I went straight to sleep on one of the bunk beds at the far end of the bunker. There were no mattresses of any kind on the beds, only a wire mesh base, but this did not worry me in the least and I was soon asleep.

When I woke up it was already morning. The Germans who had been dozing around the stove throughout the night started to go to bed. The last two sentries returned from the trench above carrying armfuls of hand grenades and a machine gun. The grenades were fully armed and ready for throwing, their end covers were removed and all one had to do was pull the string to start the fuse, but this did not seem to worry them. On arrival in the bunker they simply dropped the grenades in a corner and went straight to bed cursing the weather.

The Germans slept till late that afternoon. None of them acted as sentries in the front line during daytime. Their duties were fulfilled by an artillery observer who, while directing the fire of the field guns, also stood guard over his sleeping comrades. A long wire from the observer was connected to an alarm bell in the bunker made from a shell casing. When I climbed the steps out of the bunker in the cold but sunny morning, the first thing I saw was a pile of steel helmets. The Germans never wore these in cold weather and now they were covered by the new snow at one side of the bunker entrance. It was completely quiet outside. The Russians were probably asleep just as the Germans were. Somewhere high above I could hear the sound of an aircraft receding slowly into the distance. All of the surrounding hilly landscape was covered by fresh snow. Even the front-line trenches were half filled with snow. Everything was quiet and peaceful.

I returned to the bunker, sat down at the table and wrote a few letters. To keep warm I kept fuelling the stove with wood and coal. In mid-morning the Russians started an artillery bombardment. I could clearly hear and feel the explosions of shells above us, but it was a while before the Germans woke up. It wasn't the artillery fire that woke them but the cold air coming into the bunker through the broken transparent plastic which covered the window after a particularly near miss. One of them jumped down from his bed, cursed the Russians, and started to repair the damage. I helped him in this work and very soon the window was airtight once more. The German told me not to worry about the artillery fire – the Russians did this every morning, according to him. I cut up a few logs for the stove and sat at the table awaiting the end of the bombardment.

When the Germans started to get up the artillery fire had long since ceased to shake the bunker. The first thing they did was to melt some snow and make coffee. Next we emptied the drainage hole under the bunker floorboards, passing the bucket from hand to hand up the bunker steps. One of the Germans took me to the machine-gun position in the part of the trench line which we were to guard, so that I could see it in daytime and prepare for my spell of duty that night. The German had carried the gun with him and now put it in its place, tried a few short bursts of fire to see that it was working properly and covered the gun with a tarpaulin. About 50 yards in front of the trenches there was a thick barbed-wire fence. The German pointed out the Russian positions somewhere in the distance, but I could not see anything there – only a snow-covered ridge stretching from one low hill to another indicated where the enemy was entrenched. A couple of wires ran out from the machine gun towards the barbed-wire fence. The German told me that these wires were attached to anti-tank mines in front of our positions and we only had to pull the wires to explode the mines. After showing me where to keep the hand grenades during the night, we were preparing to return to the bunker when suddenly a Russian machine gun opened up. Its bullets chopped the snow directly above our heads and we quickly ducked into the trench. 'The bastards are awake as well as us!' the German commented laconically, and we went back along the trench to our bunker.

When it started to get dark one of the Germans went to the rear of the front line to collect our dinner: soup, bread and margarine. The rest of us took shovels and began to clear the trenches of snow. The front line here pushed forward at a sharp angle, like a sawtooth, so that the Russians were able to fire at us from two directions. In places one had to work carefully on account of Russian snipers, but these places were well known to the Germans and they warned me about the danger. After clearing the snow we cut up enough wood to keep the stove going for the night. Meanwhile the food carrier returned, we warmed up the cold soup on the stove and had our evening meal; it was then time for the first two men to go to the front line to start their sentry duty period.

I had been assigned to the second shift and went to the front-line trenches a couple of hours later. The two men already there told us that nothing had happened during their period of duty and went back to the bunker. Our two hours passed quietly as well. Now and then we shot a rocket up in the air and tried to see anything unusual in the no-man's-land between us and the Russians. Time passed very slowly. We were very cold and waited impatiently for the next two men to take over from us. On returning to the bunker we sat down at the stove and tried to keep awake for another couple of hours. Only then could we have a couple of hours sleep while other men took our place.

It was early morning when I had to leave the warm bunker and go out in the cold once more to do my second turn of sentry duty. Everything was quiet as before. Then, suddenly, a lot of rockets were sent up from the neighbouring sector of the front line, and we could hear shouting coming from the same direction. We followed suit firing off one flare after another in the air and very soon the night was as bright as day. The German with me prepared to fire the machine gun and shouted to me to get some grenades ready for throwing. A brief swish in the air was followed by the explosions of Russian mortar bombs close by. Mortar fragments and lumps of frozen earth whistled through the air and fell in front of us; the mortar fire continued unabated for a while, perhaps for a quarter of an hour. Then we heard a terrible howl to our rear and something flew hissing over our heads towards the Russians. The next moment a huge fountain of earth and snow shot up from the enemy trenches, the earth shook and a wave of air pressure hit us in the face. The Russian mortar fire stopped immediately. The German told me that the howls were made by our rockets of which the Russians were terrified. The range of these was not very great, but nevertheless they were as effective as the highest-calibre artillery shell or a large bomb. The German name for these rockets was 'Muhende Kuh' or 'Lowing Cow'. A few rifle shots followed, the flares died down and gradually everything became quiet. Somewhere in the no-man's-land we could hear the moaning of a wounded Russian which went on for a while before he too became quiet, and everything was peaceful once more by the time the sun appeared over the horizon. According to the German a Russian reconnaissance patrol had approached our trenches but had been detected and driven back losing a few men in the process. I had come through my first action at the front without firing a shot or feeling any fear. The German had not even bothered to summon his sleeping comrades from the bunker.

Chapter 9

With the 205th Division, January 1944

My next ten days at the front passed uneventfully. Sporadic fire broke out now and then, but that was about all, the cold weather probably holding back the Russians from attacking. Very soon I got used to the everyday routine of front-line life and became friendly with my German comrades. One day I was called to the German Headquarters where I had to report to Captain Lidums. He ordered me to go back to the Company's supply point and bring back some fresh mutton, explaining that his stomach could not digest the usual front-line fare and he therefore needed some fresh meat for his own use. First of all I went that evening with the German supply sled to their depot, spent the night there, and in the morning continued my way to the rear on foot, walking all day. A fresh snowstorm began as I trudged along and it was late that evening before I reached the area where units of the Latvian Legion were stationed. I slept in a Russian hut with a Latvian unit and found our Company Headquarters the next morning. During the day I got hold of a small sled, loaded it with mutton and bottles of drink provided by the Company Sergeant Major, and started on my way back to the front line the next morning, taking with me another draft of men. We finally arrived at Bojaki late that night.

A few days later, while asleep in the German bunker, I had a curious dream. In it one of the Germans came into the bunker, took his rucksack from the hook on the wall and went out saying we had to get away from there. I was therefore more than a little surprised when we were given the order to withdraw for real. My dream had come true and the person giving the order was the same German I had seen in my dream. That night we got our belongings together, shouldered our arms and began pulling out in another snowstorm. I had to carry the machine gun which was fully loaded and ready to fire at a moment's notice. It was of a new type and the Germans were not altogether familiar with it, but because I had received instruction in its use at Riga during my service with the Guards Company, I was entrusted now to carry the heavy weapon.

After a 3-mile march our section was halted and told to take up positions facing the enemy. Other men of the Company continued the withdrawal, but we had to remain behind as rearguard in case the Russians were following us. For a couple of hours we squatted in roadside ditches. We could not smoke and kept quiet in order to surprise any Russian scouting patrols. Although we were wet and very cold we needed no reminding to keep as quiet as possible. We all knew the situation we would be in if the Russians were to detect our presence.

When we finally continued on our way we were glad of the opportunity to move and get warm. We caught up with the main column of men near the river where the Company had assembled to await their turn to cross the bridge. Some Russian huts were burning here and in the red light of the flames one could see wet and tired men huddling together for warmth. A German officer jumped onto a sledge and began to explain the situation. He told us that the Russians already knew about our retreat and were cautiously following us. We should be glad it was snowing as it made visibility very poor and stopped them using their night-fighter aircraft. How near the Russians had got to us no one knew, but if we met up with them that night we should fight as the reputation of the German soldier demanded. Ending his address, the officer added that if everything went as planned, we should reach a new fortified front line in the morning.

We moved with the main column for the rest of the night, keeping a couple of hundred yards behind it, and watching carefully for any sign of Russians. But the enemy did not show up and we reached the same village where I had been warned about Russian artillery fire when I first arrived at the front. I stayed there for about a week with the Germans.

We lived in bunkers which had been dug all over the ruined village. The main front line consisted of fragmentary trenches and strongpoints. The village itself was particularly well defended with trenches and bunkers, but it had been impossible to dig very deep in the surrounding meadows due to the saturated ground. Instead of trenches the meadows were crossed by a low earth wall which contained fortified machine-gun nests, while the front of this wall was protected by the usual barbed-wire fence. The machine-gun nests were similar to the armoured turrets of tanks. Steel plates enclosed them completely and they had tightly fitting doors at the back, thus making them well protected from attackers.

Life here was peaceful. Sometimes we were bombarded by Russian artillery, but their infantry did not try to approach the new front line. Their temporary front line was situated along the hills above the river banks, and they did not dare to show themselves on the plain where they could not dig in and lacked cover. Between us and the enemy there were a couple of miles of no-man's-land where there were German listening posts whose job it was to detect any Russian attempt to approach our main front line. Even the fortified village where we lived was situated in front of the main line. One night I had to go with a group of Germans to man one of the sentry posts.

We left the village as it became dark and walked along a muddy, snow-covered road. It was thawing, all the ditches and fields were filled with water, and our boots stuck in the mud with each step. We had to be careful and keep an eye out for any Russian ambush party that might be awaiting us in the dark. A couple of hours passed while we carefully approached the site of our sentry post – a ruined Russian village. One of the Germans had been here a couple of nights ago and knew where to go. He took us to a cellar which still had a roof although the house over it had been burned to the ground. Two of the Germans took up positions with the machine gun on top of the cellar, and the rest of us went down to rest until it was our turn to go outside and stand guard. The door was covered with a piece of sacking, the air in the cellar was cold and damp, and there was a little straw on the floor on which we could sit. Some of the Germans started to make a fire in a makeshift stove made up of a few bricks, in an attempt to warm the place up, but there was no outlet for the smoke which soon filled the whole cellar making us cough and nearly choke. Everyone was so cold that we did not put the fire out, but sat around it enduring the atmosphere.

I was quite happy to get out of there and take my turn outside with one of the Germans. It was dark and silent. We kept as quiet as possible so as not to give away our position and so that we would hear any Russians nearing the village. After a while we heard the characteristic drone of a Russian aircraft. As the plane neared the village, it dropped a flare which lit up the fields around us as it descended slowly from the sky. The aircraft circled and then flew straight at us – a moment later we could hear the swish of falling bombs. As soon as we had flattened ourselves on the ground the bombs exploded nearby; steel splinters flew over us and fell into the fields with an audible splash. The aircraft did not repeat the attack and departed towards the east. I do not think that the Russians could see us from the air, although they probably knew the location of the German post in no-man's-land from information obtained otherwise. We stayed in the cellar until first light and then, wet and tired, returned to the fortified village.

A couple of days later I went with a working party to the immediate rear of the front line. We had to pull down a wooden house to provide timber for building bunkers, and also for use as firewood. In the loft of the house we found secreted some Tsarist banknotes and a certificate of service in the old Russian Army. Some Russian had hidden the money and documents, perhaps expecting the return of the old order, but now, surely, the owner must be long since lost in the turbulence of war and revolution.

Returning to the village in the evening we were told to prepare to pull back to the main front line about a mile to the west. All the time we were preparing to leave we were shelled by Russian artillery. There were rumours going round that the enemy had begun to advance and had already reached the ruined village where we had been a few nights before. Shortly before leaving the Germans sent a dozen 'Lowing Cow' rockets towards the Russian line. With a deafening roar the rockets left the ground, and one could clearly follow their flight and fall on the enemy. The following explosions shook the ground and huge fountains of smoke appeared at the place of impact. As soon as this farewell present to the Russians had been sent, we left the village. We passed carefully through our own minefields and barbed wire in front of

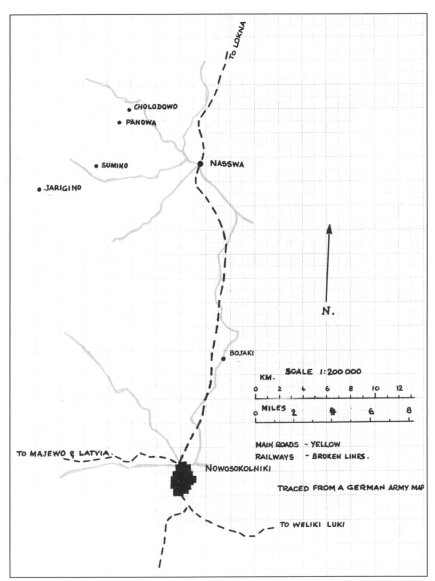

'The Nowo Sokolniki area'.

the main front line, and carried on to the rear of it, eventually stopping to spend the night in a Russian bath house.

The Russian artillery would not let us sleep and shells fell all
around the wooden house which gave us no cover worth speaking

of; we expected a direct hit at any moment. When a German soldier appeared at the door and asked if there was anyone familiar with the new-pattern machine gun, I replied straight away. The Germans could not understand my volunteering for service in the front line, but I wanted to get away from there – to me, the front-line bunkers seemed a much safer place to be in.

I followed the German to the front-line trench and had to wait a while for my orders outside a dugout occupied by the German unit commander. At last the officer came out of the bunker and thanked me for my offer to serve under him. However, he could not take me on and told me that all Latvians had to go to the rear of the front line in the morning and report to their Legion units. I could spend the night there. The German soldier took me into the bunker, showed me where to sleep and wished me goodnight. I slept well all night and even the continuous Russian artillery fire did not disturb me much.

When I left the front line the next morning the Russian artillery was still busy, and as a parting gift sent three shells after me. They came without any warning and fell quite close to where I was. I did not have time to throw myself down, but I was lucky – the shells buried themselves in the frozen earth without exploding! My luck was certainly in, I thought, as I went on my way, thus ending my service with the German 205th Division.

Chapter 10

Return to the 32nd Latvian Regiment and Action near Cholodowo, Early February 1944

I left the German 205th Division and returned to the Latvian Legion at the end of January 1944. We were stationed in a Russian village well clear of the front line. While waiting for further orders we spent a couple of peaceful days there and received the monthly ration of drinks and cigarettes. Some reinforcements arrived from Latvia, among whom was a corporal who was always telling tales about his own bravery. He used to drink all night with his friends and his voice could be heard non-stop extolling his virtues and fearlessness in the face of the enemy.

At last the order came to prepare to leave. I went to a neighbouring village with a couple of my friends to try to obtain a sled on which we could transport our rucksacks during the march. We found the sled alright, but there was a snag: it was already being loaded up by an elderly Russian couple in their house. The Russians begged us to leave the sled with them. They were so old that without it they would not get far, so we became soft-hearted and returned home empty handed.

When we began marching early the next morning the weather had become warm. It was thawing and even those who had managed to obtain a sled for their packs did not fare much better than those without one. Our feet became wet and the belts of our rucksacks cut into our shoulders. We had to stop frequently, but it was impossible to sit or lie down and rest as the ground was too wet, and we had to stand around waiting to move on.

Late in the morning of 4 February 1944 we reached a railway station (probably Nasswa) and assembled in the station square. This was one of the main stations on this line and it even had a high water tower for replenishing the passing locomotives. Thinking that the march had ended we were in high spirits.

'We've finished with foot-slogging now,' shouted one Legionnaire. 'After getting into the wagons we'll be driven along like lords!' Bottles of drink started to pass from hand to hand and as their contents diminished our spirits improved further. And then, around dinner time, we received another order – to prepare for battle. The officers tried to pacify us by saying that it would be easy. We only had to see off some weak Russian units which had broken across our intended route before we could continue on our way. We were told to leave our packs in a heap in the station square, to be collected after the action. I was left with only my food pouch, with some bread and meat paste in it, and the water bottle which I had filled with strong tangerine-flavoured liqueur. I had a packet of tobacco in my pocket for smoking.

We began the march to the front line in a long column on both sides of the road. Passing through a village we met German soldiers hiding between the houses and in the doorways. They seemed glad to see us and shouted, 'The SS are advancing!' waving to us at the same time.

We did not have to go far. A mile further on we passed through another village and spread out in extended order in the fields beyond it. About 400 yards in front of us were some low wooded hills, on top of which were a few German tanks. The Russians were supposed to be behind the hills in the direction the tank guns were pointing. The snow was wet and we did not fancy the prospect of digging in, especially as there seemed no reason to do so at the time. Everything was quiet in front of us and the German tanks were protecting us from any surprise attack.

We stayed in the field until late afternoon hoping that we would have to return to the railway station and collect our belongings, but were disappointed.[1] When we started to march once more we were heading in the opposite direction. It became dark and we were still on the road walking through snowbound country.

Our feet were wet, we were tired and cold, and we did not get much rest during the short halts as we had to stay standing. Very soon we were shivering with cold and were nearly falling asleep on our feet when we started on the next leg of our journey.

As we approached a village we were met by a couple of shots, followed by two flares ascending into the night sky. Without any order being given we ran off the road and formed up on both sides of it. In a moment our machine guns were in position and the ammunition sled was brought up across the snowbound fields. We were ready. Our eyes scanned the country in front of us, our weapons fully prepared to open fire on the still invisible enemy. For a while nothing happened, and then the order came to regroup on the road to continue the march. The flares had been fired by a German detachment guarding the village and we were told that the enemy was still a long way away.

Our legs ached even more after the latest incident and the road seemed to be without end. We were warned that anyone remaining behind might well fall into the hands of the Russians and could expect to be shot on the spot after being tortured, but we were so tired and cold that this did not seem the worst that could happen. Sleep and rest were the most important things to us at that moment.

We were promised some rest when at last we stopped near a village. After standing at the roadside for some time we were allowed to enter a house which was already overflowing with Legionnaires who had arrived ahead of us. Now the room was so full it was quite impossible to move. I managed to find a space near a window and sat down. I was lucky. The inhabitants had already managed to kill a pig and there was a whole bowl of melted fat on the window right in front of me. I found some bread in my food container, helped myself to the dripping and the meal tasted marvellous. After eating I went to sleep straight away in the narrow space.

We were not allowed to sleep for long. A shouted order made us get up, stagger over other cursing and swearing bodies, and line up outside on the road. It was still dark. We could not see any sign of the approaching morning and the biting wind made us shiver with cold. We had just lined up and were ready to start marching when an officer ran out of the house. A wristwatch had been stolen from him during our stay and now he accused us, or rather one of us, of having committed the crime. He asked the culprit to step forward and shamed us about such behaviour under the circumstances, threatened us with court-martial proceedings, but no one offered to return his watch. 'Do not get excited, Dad,' someone whispered behind me. 'You will not see your watch again.' Another soldier added in a hushed voice, 'Searching won't help you either – the watch will have been thrown away in the snow and no one will have it! Better get back in the hut and go to sleep!'

After taking all our names the officer left and we again started marching through the night along the fresh snow-covered road. After we'd been going for some time, we stopped by a copse at the roadside. A short while later an officer told us that we would have to take up defensive positions here and indicated where these positions were to be. We climbed into a partially dug trench and had to start clearing it of snow straight away. There were no bunkers here. We had to get as comfortable as possible under the open sky, and although tired, we had to be watchful because no one really knew how far the enemy was from us.

We waited impatiently for the morning of 4 February 1944. After a while the eastern sky turned red and the sun came up so that we could see where we were. Directly in front of our trenches there was a deep, wooded ravine with a small stream at the bottom of it. The other side of the ravine was a little lower than ours. Beyond that was a series of fields rising slowly, and behind them was a village about 400 yards from us. Everything was quiet in front of us and we could not see any signs of life in the village itself. We were ordered to keep quiet, the lighting of fires was strictly forbidden and we were to keep under cover.

To get warm a couple of men started to dig a communication trench to the rear of the line and came across a buried store of household goods, hidden by the local people. There was not much of value among the things they found. The hoard contained pots and pans, knives, forks and some beautifully made coloured and lacquered wooden spoons. We also found a barrel of peas and some corn. We crunched some of the peas and I passed around my bottle of liqueur. The strong spirit helped somewhat to keep out the cold. Around dinner time we were visited by the Regimental Commander who approached us along the road which ran along the rear of the line. One of the NCOs was about to jump out of the trench to report, but was stopped – the enemy might see him, he was told by one of the officers.

That afternoon section after section of us were taken out of the front line and allowed to rest and get warm in a village before returning to the positions. There was a hot stove in the house appointed for this purpose, and we could sit on the straw-covered floor and dry out our socks and boots. I cooked some of the Russian dried peas and they tasted really good with some dripping. The last thing I did was fill my bottle with hot coffee and then it was time to return to the trenches.

When the evening came and it was quite dark a group of Legionnaires arrived in the line from the rear. They were led by a Corporal and their task was to reconnoitre the village of Panowo on the other side of the ravine. The Corporal asked for some matches and promised to burn down a large barn at the end of the village which provided good cover for the enemy. Having been given some matches, they all disappeared in the dark towards the village. Everything remained quiet for some time and then we saw flames shooting out of the barn roof – the Corporal had accomplished his task. The fire lit up no-man's-land for a long time but we could not see any sign of the enemy there and the village remained quiet. After an uneventful night we were cold again, although we kept a constant watch for the approach of any Russians, but they did not come.

Around dinner time on 6 February 1944 we were taken out of the line and replaced by another unit. We were told that we could rest somewhere in the rear of the front line. We spent the rest of the day in a wooden village hut. I had not had any sleep for three nights and after eating some of the food I had with me, I went to sleep on the straw-covered floor. When it was quite dark I was awakened by the Platoon Commander who told me that I and another man named Liepa had to go on sentry duty. We had a quick drink of hot coffee and then the Sergeant took us to the place where we had to take up our positions – a trench at the top of a hill about 300 yards back from our front line. Our duty was to act as a second line of defence and we were armed with a machine gun. We had to ensure that no Russians passed through the fragmentary front-line trenches to attack them from the rear, and we were to fire over the heads of our own men if there was a frontal attack by the enemy.

The night was clear and we were very cold standing motionless in the trench. To keep some of the cold out we covered ourselves with some flax which we had found in one of the surrounding fields. While one of us kept watch the other tried to sleep in the bottom of the trench. We changed places every half hour, but during our watch did not see anything of the enemy. Everything was very quiet except for the sound of Russian aircraft flying over at frequent intervals. As they circled us one of them, like a great black bird, crossed the face of the moon. It seemed as if they were trying to discover the position of our front line. They did not drop any bombs, only their flares descended slowly, lighting up the countryside.

A couple of hours later the next two men arrived to start their turn of duty and we returned to the village. Just as we were about to go to sleep, everyone was alerted and told to prepare for action. Led by an officer we were to go to Cholodowo and support our troops there during the expected Russian attack. We lined up outside and were given extra ammunition and hand grenades. I had to carry two boxes of machine-gun ammunition, a heavy load which soon tired my arms.

While marching through the village we were surprised by heavy artillery fire. The shells exploded all around us and to take cover we ran into one of the Russian houses. The house was empty and we were able to see from the light of the full moon. We were just about to leave the house during a lull in the shelling when a couple of shells exploded right outside the door. We ducked down and could hear the shell fragments smacking into the outside walls. Behind us a frightened voice said that the safest place would be in the bread oven. It was the Corporal who had bragged about his own bravery. He actually tried to get into the oven, but followed us meekly when we abandoned the place.

We left the village behind us and began to walk towards Cholodowo along a dirt road across the fields. Ahead of us we could hear the frequent explosions of shells and mortar bombs. We were right in the middle of the open fields, approximately 300 yards from Cholodowo, when the mortar fire was redirected onto us. Running off the road we lay down to escape the bombardment. I placed one of the ammunition boxes on either side of my head, and all we could do was wait for the fire to cease, but we did not receive any orders to move on and the mortar bombs continued to explode uncomfortably close all around us. From the village in front of us we could hear continuous rifle fire, the rattling of machine guns and the battle cries of attacking Russians, followed by the firing of numerous machine guns and the explosions of hand grenades. The shouting of the Russians became feebler and ceased altogether, but the characteristic sound of our 'bone saws' continued unabated. The Russians had been beaten back. The mortar fire on us became sporadic, we assembled in small groups in the field and finally entered the village of Cholodowo where the firing was still going on.

We went from house to house trying to find our officer. There were some German assault guns and tanks in the village, but we could not find anyone who knew where our Lieutenant and the rest of our unit were assembled. During our search we entered one of the wooden houses, but it was empty and full of driven snow. Cold gusts of air blew in every time the assault gun fired outside in the orchard and the remaining fragments of glass fell from the windows.

In the end we came across some men of our unit who told us that the assembly point was a barn on the outskirts of the village. When we arrived there we saw in one of the corners some light coming from a candle. Some men sat around our officer who had been wounded during our approach to the village. This meant that we no longer had a leader. A couple of men had organized the officer's transport to the rear and we followed him. Now that the enemy attack had been repulsed without our help we had no intention of getting involved in the fighting around the village. We reached our village without any further problems and went to sleep.

Notes

1 We did not recover the rucksacks with our personal belongings which we had left in the station's square. I heard later that they had been burned to prevent their falling into the hands of the enemy. The most valuable thing I lost was a golden ring with a blue stone in it which had once belonged to my mother's mother and had been given to me when going to war. I also lost my underclothes and socks which would have been useful in the days that followed.

Chapter 11

The Attack on Panowo,
7 February 1944

It was fine and sunny as dawn broke on 7 February 1944. It was already late morning by the time I got up and straight after breakfast we received the order to go to a neighbouring village to obtain extra ammunition and hand grenades. We were to prepare for battle and as there was an unlimited supply of ammunition in the village everyone could take as much as they wanted. Besides a hundred extra rounds of rifle ammunition I took with me three rifle grenades which could also be thrown, and were much easier to carry than the usual type of hand grenades.

Around dinner time we left the village marching along a road which was at the rear of the front line and behind the hill I had guarded the previous night. My companion of the previous night, Liepa, was with me again at this time. In the morning I had been appointed to command a section and thus did not have to carry the heavy ammunition boxes. We could not see the front line which was hidden by the hill, but we could see a number of aircraft in that direction diving one after another to release their bombs. It all seemed to be taking place some distance from us, but suddenly we heard the sound of numerous aircraft engines approaching us from the front. We ran off the road and dispersed in the bushes on both sides of it just as the planes appeared flying low over the hill. We could clearly see the black German crosses on their wings and without delay assembled once more on the road to continue on our way. The planes were German 'Stuka' dive-bombers which had been bombing Russian artillery positions and their front line, and we were mighty pleased to see them.

We marched a little further, turned to the left and reached the crest of the hill. The other side of the hill descended slowly to a ravine along which were our front line trenches. The hillside was covered with a sparse growth of bushes and we were ordered to spread out among them approximately 300 yards behind the front line. This indicated that we would be in the second wave of the attack. Beyond the ravine we could clearly see the village of Panowo which was our objective. The occasional bullet whizzed past us and a few shells landed in our midst throwing up clouds of powdery snow. We were not under heavy fire, but to prepare for any eventuality we were told to lie down. We could hear continuous rifle and machine-gun fire from our right where, since that morning, the Germans had been trying to take the same village we were about to attack. Several German attempts had already failed to drive the enemy from the village and even as we awaited our turn, they tried once more. We could hear their battle cries and watched the snow and smoke shooting up from the explosions of shells. After a short while the noise of battle cleared, and dive-bombers immediately came back on the scene and bombed the village of Panowo.

We had been on the snow-covered hillside for a couple of hours, and the moment of our attack was now at hand. The roar of the aircraft engines, their howling dives and the explosions of their bombs merged into a terrible din. The earth shook, snow fell from the branches of the bushes and without an order all of us got up to check our weapons and stretch our stiffening legs. We had a grand view of the bombing. The village of Panowo soon became enveloped in a cloud of smoke and fog. We could only see the roofs of houses and tops of trees above which the bombs threw up fountains of earth and smoke. The bombing ended abruptly; straight away a line of Legionnaires left the front-line trench and started to go forward. We followed the first wave, keeping a distance of 300 yards between them and us. I saw our Company Commander, Second Lieutenant Jauntirans among us. His clothes were only semi-military as he was wearing a fur coat and a hat with freely swinging ear flaps.

The Russians held their fire as we began to advance – it seemed that they had not recovered from the bombing, but this did not last

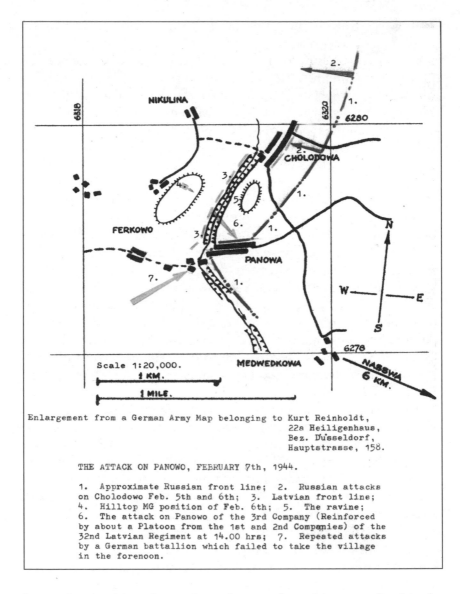

Enlargement from a German Army Map belonging to Kurt Reinholdt,
22a Heiligenhaus,
Bez. Düsseldorf,
Hauptstrasse, 158.

THE ATTACK ON PANOWO, FEBRUARY 7th, 1944.

1. Approximate Russian front line; 2. Russian attacks
on Cholodowo Feb. 5th and 6th; 3. Latvian front line;
4. Hilltop MG position of Feb. 6th; 5. The ravine;
6. The attack on Panowo of the 3rd Company (Reinforced
by about a Platoon from the 1st and 2nd Companies) of the
32nd Latvian Regiment at 14.00 hrs; 7. Repeated attacks
by a German battallion which failed to take the village
in the forenoon.

long. On reaching the ravine a burst of machine-gun fire hit the
snow directly in front of me and rifle bullets were already whizzing
past us. We jumped over our front-line trenches, slid down the
steep bank of the ravine, crossed the narrow frozen stream and,
after climbing the opposite bank, continued to advance on the
village. The sloping ground covered us from direct fire, but we
came under fire instead from Russian mortars. In front of us

we could hear the battle cries of our first wave, some confused and nervous shooting and the explosions of hand grenades. After a short while these noises ceased and only the mortars continued the fire on us. We passed their zone of fire and reached the village without any further trouble.

There was still confusion in the village. The Russians had just run away after resisting, and our men had not yet reorganized. Russian bullets were still smacking into the walls of the houses and whizzed past our ears as we searched the village, running from house to house and keeping behind them for cover from enemy fire. But we did not find any more Russians, who had left the village in a great hurry. In one of the huts we found a cauldron of cabbage and pork still boiling on the stove. We also found a Russian anti-tank rifle outside, with its barrel camouflaged by being bound with a white field bandage. Shouts from my men made me look in the direction they indicated. There, just visible in the fog, I could see someone crawling away in the direction the Russians had taken. I could not distinguish or identify his uniform and shouted in Latvian to stop. When there was no answer I aimed my rifle and fired. The stranger quickened his movements, my next shots did not appear to hit him and he disappeared into the fog.

With the enemy continuing to bring down fire on the village, I saw a bearded Legionnaire clutching a bleeding shoulder as he walked cheerfully to the rear. 'See you again in Latvia!' he shouted. We heard stories from the men of our first wave while taking the village. Someone had run up to a hut with a Russian machine gun sticking through its window. The machine gunner had not seen his approach and had continued firing. The Legionnaire had simply grabbed the gun's barrel and wrenched the weapon from the hands of the surprised Russian. Another of our men, a machine gunner, had used his gun like a rifle during the attack, kicking up the long belt of ammunition with his knee! I personally did not do much shooting during this attack. While approaching the village across the fields I fired once into a loft window where I glimpsed some movement, later firing at the escaping Russian who I probably missed. That was all.

An order came for the second wave of Legionnaires to leave the village and form a second line of defence in the field which we had just crossed. I assembled my section and spread them out at the indicated place. The men began to dig in making shallow holes in the snow. I joined Liepa, my friend of the last few days, in his hole and we both continued to dig for a while. We were under continuous mortar fire and could clearly hear the mortars being fired off, followed by their swish in the air as they fell and the explosions all around us. Liepa went to the village to look for some straw to put in the bottom of our trench to make it more comfortable. He returned with an armful of straw and sat down on the edge of the shallow hole watching me trying to make it deeper. The mortar bombs were now landing ever closer, the snow from their explosions filled the air and we could hear the sound of shrapnel flying past us. I urged Liepa to get down into the trench and even as he moved to follow my advice there was the short swish of a falling mortar bomb followed by a deafening explosion very close to us.

I felt a powerful blow in my back. Liepa fell over me and stayed there without moving. My mouth was filled with something warm and salty. I coughed and spat blood onto the snow. I got onto my hands and knees with some difficulty and shouted for stretcher bearers. I had to spit out another couple of mouthfuls of blood and then the bleeding stopped. Liepa seemed to be dead. He lay across me without moving and, turning my head, I could see that his felt boots were holed in many places with mortar bomb fragments. He had shielded me with his body from most of the fragments from the mortar bomb. My body felt strangely tired all over and although there was no pain, I did not try to move as I waited for the arrival of the stretcher bearers, trying to figure out where I was wounded. I hoped that I had not been hit in the stomach, knowing that such wounds were often fatal, but at that moment I did not fear death and was sure of my ability to survive.

A while later several of my men arrived at the trench, lifted Liepa off me, took off his overcoat and placed me on it. Then four of them grabbed the coat and carried me to the wounded assembly point. I was laid down at the side of a haystack and told to keep still while waiting for the transport. There were several other wounded men already there, most of whom lay in the snow; only one sat up leaning on the haystack nursing a wounded arm.

We were still being mortared. As evening approached, the waiting and the explosions of mortar bombs seemed to be endless. In the twilight and fog we could still hear the mortars firing. Every time I heard the approach of the next batch of the accursed bombs

I tried to flatten myself as much as possible, then all I could do was trust my good luck. I was unable to take proper cover and was at considerable risk of being hit a second time. The Legionnaire who had been sitting up was hit by shrapnel once more and collapsed moaning in the snow. My feet were freezing. With the approach of night the cold became bitter and my hands began to freeze as well. By this time the mortaring had slowed down somewhat. The full red moon, shining through the fog, had climbed well up the eastern sky when transport for the wounded finally arrived.

The sled was driven slowly, but still shook on the poor road and the wounded moaned in pain. My chest ached now at the slightest movement, but I had to bear it until the end of the journey.

We reached a village where we were unloaded and laid down on the straw-covered floor in one of the houses. It was warm and quiet here. I was very tired and cold, and soon went to sleep. When I awoke I could hear the sound of aircraft engines outside, the explosions of bombs and the firing of machine guns. The medical orderlies took cover by lying on the floor beside us and along the walls as they waited for the air attack to end. Once all was quiet again we were offered mugs of hot coffee, which I refused. I heard one of the medical orderlies whisper to his mate as they moved on, 'I don't think this one will live.' I found his remark quite amusing as I felt well and just wanted to sleep. I was terribly tired and to sleep in safety seemed more important than anything. 'I will not die,' I told myself and fell asleep once more.

Part III

Recovery

Chapter 12

Hospital and Home Leave, February to June 1944

The next day I was placed on a stretcher, lifted into an ambulance and driven to another village. I felt much better now and spent the day sleeping on a warm bread oven in a room full of wounded soldiers. I was able to eat some biscuits, drink some coffee and even ventured outside to the lavatory. The bright winter's day dazzled my eyes but I could not find the lavatory and did what I had to do in a nearby barn.

After another long ride in an ambulance I arrived at a small Russian town with a field hospital. Here at last I was put in a bed and was examined thoroughly by a doctor. I was carried into the operating theatre, undressed and a wide band of plaster was put around my chest. I expected to remain there for further treatment, but a couple of days later I was driven to the railway station and placed on a train for the wounded. There was not much comfort on this train. We were carried in cattle trucks and had to lie on the straw-covered floor. There was a stove in the middle but it was still cold in the corners of the wagon. Very soon the train left the station for an unknown destination.

All the wounded in my wagon were German – as the only Latvian among them I was able to use my knowledge of German to good advantage. We organized the duties of keeping the stove alight among the more lightly wounded and watched the outside world go by through a narrow gap in the door. The train travelled very slowly as there were partisans in the region who often blew up trains and loosened the bolts on the line, thus hoping to derail trains. The track was enclosed by a barbed-wire fence on each side and there were numerous guard towers along the line. The country-side was thickly wooded and we seldom saw an open plain. To keep the cold air out we did not spend too much time at the door, but mostly kept it shut so that we could sleep.

When we awoke the train was stationary and we could hear voices outside. We opened the door and saw that we were in a large railway station. A railwayman told us that we were in Pskow. Some Red Cross sisters came along the platform with a trolley and started to distribute hot soup, food, bottles of drink, chocolate and - cigarettes. Some of the more seriously wounded men were taken off the train here to receive immediate medical attention, and we continued our journey.

The buildings of Pskow were soon left behind us and we travelled once more through snow-covered fields and dark pine forests. Some of us slept in the corners of the wagon, the rest sat around the stove drinking vodka, smoking and speculating about the ultimate destination of the train. When the train finally stopped I opened the door. It was early morning. Our wagon had stopped on a crossing and on the road I could see a woman in a sled loaded with milk churns. I asked her in German where we were but she shook her head. When I repeated the question in Latvian she told me we were near Gulbene, which was good news and I secretly hoped we would be going to Riga. I did not feel so well now: my head ached and I felt very hot.

When the train next stopped I saw that we were in a small town. The station had the name Madona and some of the wounded were already being unloaded from the train. It was Sunday, 13 February 1944, and was a bright, sunny morning.

Somewhere a church bell tolled softly. People walked slowly along a street parallel with the railway line in groups of men and women, looking towards the train and talking among themselves. Everything that winter morning was peaceful and quiet. The town slept enclosed by white fields, and even our suffering and the activity at the station could not disturb the rural Sunday calm.

The train was a long one, the unloading of the wounded progressed slowly and it was evening when my turn came to leave the railway wagon. The medical orderlies laid me on a stretcher, lifted it into an ambulance and after a short drive I was at the hospital. A German doctor examined me briefly and then sent all the lightly wounded for a bath and de-lousing. Soon I was clean and dressed in hospital uniform before being carried on a stretcher to the operating theatre, where three bright lights shone above three operating tables. Tired doctors examined the wounded and changed the dressings at the same time. My wide band of plaster was removed and replaced by a narrower band of sticking plaster. Only now, for the first time, I was told that I had a shell fragment in one of my lungs. In the operating theatre I was registered on the roll of the hospital by a German official and only then, late that evening, I was transported to the Lung Department of the hospital and placed in a clean bed. A Red Cross sister offered me supper – a milk pudding – but I was too tired to bother to eat. My head was aching and I was short of breath. It was late in the night before I could get to sleep.

The next morning I felt just as bad. My head ached, I was short of breath and tortured by unending thirst. There were about ten men in the room and I was the only Latvian among the Germans. I trusted German doctors much more than their Latvian colleagues. I was told that the chief surgeon was a famous professor from the University Clinic of Vienna and that many of the sisters were of Austrian origin.

During the first day nothing happened. The famous surgeon came to visit us in the morning and made a brief examination of each man. He was a middle-aged man, intelligent looking and dark of eye and face. He tapped and listened to my chest, the sister noted his instructions on a pad, and then he went to the next bed.

The following day I was carried down to the X-ray Department and examined there. An X-ray photograph was taken at the same time which I secretly managed to get hold of and have a look at the damage. I could clearly see the shell fragment lodged in my right lung. I could also see the doctor's writing on my chart. His diagnosis was: 'Cherry-sized shell fragment in the right lung. Central region, within the lung.' My lung was filled with blood, and the resulting pressure had moved my heart tightly against the ribs on the left side of my chest. During his visit later the doctor once more examined the photograph and told the sister to take me to the operating theatre the next morning.

When I arrived at the theatre the next day the surgeon had just finished operating on a wounded soldier who was still on one of the tables. He was unconscious and pale, while the doctor slowly and unconcernedly washed his hands preparing to deal with me. First of all he asked me how I felt, and then gave instructions to the theatre sister who made me sit up on the next table and began to paint my back with brown antiseptic. I asked her what they intended to do with me, but she would not tell me a thing. She only laughed and told me to wait and see. Having finished cleaning me up the sister pushed a small trolley to my side on which I could see various instruments, among them, which caused me some concern, a simply enormous syringe. I did not have much time to speculate about the purpose of this monster. The surgeon arrived and told me: 'Don't worry, we only want to get some of the blood out of your chest cavity', and then he set to work. He ordered me to bend forward and cross my arms, then gave me a local anaesthetic to freeze an area of my back. After that he pushed the large needle of the syringe into my back between the ribs. I did not feel any pain, and looking back could see the syringe filling with dark blood. The doctor turned a valve on the needle connector and through a side outlet emptied the blood into a kidney shaped dish. A total of about three pints of blood were removed and I was returned to my room.

I could breathe much easier now, and a couple of days later the high temperature and headache eased. I had started to recover. The doctor told me that he intended to leave the shell fragment in my lung and allow it to become coated with lime, for which I was given calcium and vitamin C tablets. I went to the operating theatre twice more and had another pint of blood removed from my chest – that was all the treatment I needed to recover.

One day a dead man was carried into our room. At least the man certainly looked dead when he was brought in by the orderlies and put on one of the beds. He was very thin and his head was completely shaven; his face was of a grey colour and he smelled horribly of decay. A rubber tube protruded from under his stretcher ending in a bottle which was half full of a yellow discharge. When the man had been placed in his bed we could see that the tube was attached to his chest and served to drain the lung cavity of pus. In a weak voice he told us that he had served in a German penal company close to the front line building fortifications and digging trenches. He had not been wounded but had abscesses in his lungs. The food had been very poor in the company and because of this he had lost a lot of weight. Once in hospital the man soon recovered. He managed to eat everything left over from our meals and still asked the sisters for more. He soon put on weight, his abscesses stopped discharging and the terrible smell which filled the room every time his bottle was changed disappeared.

All the men in the room had been wounded in the lungs. My neighbour was a soldier with half a dozen shell splinters in his chest, while some of the Germans had been in the hospital for some time. I got to know a Latvian girl who worked in the hospital and she told me that I was the only Latvian soldier in the whole building. She brought me some local newspapers so that I could read once more in my own language. We had plenty to eat at the hospital and were quite often given vodka, wine and cigarettes. I had not smoked since I had been wounded and did not drink so that very soon I had saved several hundred cigarettes and had accumulated quite a collection of bottles in my locker.

Madona was a small town in central Latvia and the hospital was housed in the local school, the largest building in the town. My second-storey window offered me a wide view of the countryside – I could now see snow-covered fields, a distant forest and a couple of church spires.

One day in mid-March I had an unexpected visitor. I had written to my mother in Riga on my first day in hospital and told her what had happened. She had obtained the necessary travel permit and without letting me know arrived at Madona. When she came to my bed her eyes filled with tears. After kissing me she said that I looked very pale and thin and asked whether the food was all right in the hospital. She had been worried in case I had lied to her and not told her everything. 'I can see for myself that you have nothing missing and will be able to sleep better now,' she said and started to unpack all the good things she had brought with her. She had baked a special cake for me and urged me to eat it to speed my recovery. We talked of home and the people there so that the time passed quickly. I was still unable to talk much and was soon out of breath, so my mother did most of the talking. When she left me for the station she took with her many of the bottles of vodka I had saved up and a thousand cigarettes. Such things were of great value on the black market and she would be able to exchange them for food items in short supply.

Time passed slowly after my mother's visit, especially as I had to stay in bed. I still had a headache and therefore could not read much. I spent my days listening to the Germans talking about their lives at home and their adventures in the front line. Late one evening we heard a commotion outside and a short while later the orderlies carried into our room a big man who was quite naked. He was placed in the bed next to mine and I soon found out that he was a Latvian. He had been wounded while driving over a bridge near Madona by a mine which had been placed by a partisan. We did not talk much, just enough to obtain the inform- ation needed by the ward sister. I could clearly hear the bubbling sound of blood in his chest as he breathed, and I could also see that he had a large hole in his back which was covered by a bloody bandage. The sister told me to watch the wounded man during the night and to call her if he started to move or thrash about with his arms. While I was asleep the new man got up and left the room – I was woken up as the sister and one of the night-duty men brought him back into the room. He had lost his dressing and bright red blood was running down his back. The night orderly had caught him when he had gone downstairs and tried to leave the building. The sister put the man to bed once more and replaced his dressing, hoping for the best.

In the early hours of the morning the man's heavy breathing could be heard by everyone in the room and none of us could sleep any more. Later, as the nurses were making the beds, the wounded man started to breathe irregularly and roll about in bed. I called the sister and she gave the man an injection, then stood by his bed, holding his wrist to feel his pulse until the breathing stopped altogether and the unknown Latvian died. The sister crossed his arms, closed his eyes and pulled the sheet over his face. Then she went to tell the male nurses to carry the corpse away to the mortuary. So simple was death that Palm Sunday morning of 26 March 1944, with the sun shining and a new spring approaching.

In the afternoon of the same day we were surprised by unexpected visitors – local Home Guards and pupils of the school in which we were now housed. The school chorus sang some Latvian folk songs in the corridor and then came around the beds distributing presents. When the children got to know that I was a Latvian they left by my bedside a whole heap of good things – mostly home-baked cakes, buns and sweets. I shared these gifts with the Germans in the room and most of the cakes were eaten by the German with the lung abscesses whose appetite was still enormous.

During the next week many more wounded soldiers than usual arrived at the hospital from the front. Beds were placed in the corridors to make room for the new arrivals, but this was still not enough. An order came for the lighter wounded to prepare to be moved to some wooden huts in the suburbs of the town. I had to leave the hospital with these men and so went to the storeroom to look for my uniform. It was easy to put on the jacket which only had a small hole in the back where the shell splinter had entered, but I had to make do with any other items of clothing that fitted. I walked without any help to the huts. It was a bright early spring day outside. I was half blinded by the snow and felt dizzy in the fresh, cool air, but I was also glad that I could already walk unsupported and because the end of winter was in sight.

We had a lot more freedom while living in the wooden huts. All of us had our uniforms and could go outside any time to sit in the warm sunshine. Life was peaceful and it seemed that the war and the front line were very far away. But this was an illusion and the enemy soon reminded us of his presence even there. On the night of Maundy Thursday to Good Friday I was awakened by the sound of explosions. The wooden boards of the hut were shaking, the window panes rattling and all of a sudden all the men in the room were sitting up in their beds. I put on my uniform and went outside in the foggy moonlit night. I could hear that the noise was coming from some distance away and we were therefore in no immediate danger. The distant glare of flares and the sound of explosions were to the east where, unbeknown to me at the time, Rezekne was destroyed – a town approximately 50 miles away.

During my time in the huts I was often visited by Gaida, one of the schoolgirls I had befriended when we were still in the school and the local people came with presents. She brought me books to read and we often sat for hours on a bench outside the huts and talked – a pleasant way to pass the time. I had nothing better to do and she was an interesting girl. I wanted her to become my 'Girl at Home', a term coined during the war years, and to give me a photograph of herself. This she would not do and there was a simple reason for this. There had recently been a case in Madona of a local girl's photograph being found pinned to a telegraph pole with an unflattering note underneath and Gaida did not wish this to happen to her. Her father had a shop in the town and was a man of some importance in the community. No arguments of mine could persuade her otherwise. I couldn't really blame her – she had only known me a short time.

On 20 April – Hitler's birthday – every man was given a bottle of German champagne as a present, but it was a weak brew. I drank mine like lemonade and didn't feel any effect. It was a beautiful day, the sun was dazzling and most of the snow had already disappeared. When I went for a walk along the riverside I could see that the snowdrops were just beginning to flower. In the mornings the larks greeted the rising sun with their song and during the daytime the fields steamed in the warm sun. A new spring and summer were coming – a summer when the fate of Latvia would be decided and when many would lose everything they possessed and would leave their native land.

A couple of days later, on 22 April, I was unexpectedly told to prepare for transfer to another hospital. Within an hour I was in the station and on the train when Gaida and her friend came running along the platform. They had just got to know I was leaving and brought a bunch of daffodils as a parting gift. We sat on the side of the embankment until it was time for the train to leave, feeling sad and miserable. During my short time here we had become good friends. When the train left the station the two girls were left waving their arms in the air as a final farewell from Madona. Soon one of the huge forests near Madona enclosed the train on both sides and I was alone once more with the Germans.

The journey went on all night. In the grey light of early morning I could see that the train was passing through countryside familiar to me. We were heading from Jelgava towards Lithuania and I could just make out in the distance my grandfather's farm Buki, enclosed by forest.

Was I really being taken to a hospital in Germany? The thought

persisted as the train crossed the Lithuanian border, but soon afterwards slowed down and stopped at Sauli. The unloading of the
wounded started right away and then I knew that I would remain
here, quite close to my native land.

During my month-long stay in the hospital in Sauli I met many of
my comrades, Latvians from my own unit. Most of them had been
wounded during the heavy fighting in March. Compared to their
wounds, mine was quite light. My mates told me about the March
battles when the front was covered by dead Russians. The
Company Commander had been very proud of his men. During
quieter moments he had walked along the trenches dealing out
cigarettes and encouraging the men by saying, 'Let them have it
next time you see them moving.' He hated the Russians and had no
feelings for their wounded or dying.

I had recovered so well that I was given various duties in connection with the running of the hospital. Quite often I had to
interpret when a Latvian soldier arrived from the front or another
hospital. A couple of times each week I and another of those
convalescing were put on night duty in place of the night sister. We
had to wake her any time something serious required her presence,
but otherwise the whole building was in our hands. We were
permitted to stay in the hospital kitchen during the night and had
the opportunity to obtain extra food. We fried eggs and in the
morning, returning to the ward, our pockets were stuffed with
biscuits and dried fruit. The following day we were allowed to sleep
until dinner time. I knew very well that I was to leave the hospital
shortly and was not surprised when I received my discharge papers.
I did not have to report to my unit immediately but was given
another month's convalescence leave. My papers stated that I was
on leave from 20 May 1944 to 18 June 1944 and could spend the
time as I pleased. I was also given the necessary food coupons for
this period and went to the station to catch the train to Riga.

It is hard to describe one's feelings being on leave at such a time.
In the beginning one is glad to be free of the discipline and among
one's own people, far from the dangers of the front line. And yet
at the same time one is subconsciously aware all the while that time
is passing and the day approaching when one will have to return
to army life. At the start of one's leave that day seems to be so far

away that it causes little concern. Later the days pass one after another in quick succession, the moment of parting draws nearer and one is helpless and unable to stop the flow of time. More than ever I felt this helpless inevitability that time as the new summer began. I sensed that this summer would be the last of its kind for my relatives when they could live and work peacefully. I somehow knew that they would soon be living under a different rule in fear of their belongings and their lives.

At the beginning of June I spent a week in Riga and during that time managed to get to Madona to visit Gaida and the hospital. Only a few of my former room mates remained but our ward sister was still there.

Part IV

Return to the Russian Front

Chapter 13

Return to the Front in Russia, July 1944

After my convalescent leave, I was sent first of all to Jelgava, which was where the Legion Assembly Unit for soldiers returning from hospital was situated. The men were sorted out here and then posted to various units depending on their condition. I stayed there a couple of days and then, with about a company of Legionnaires, went to Rundale. Arriving late in the evening we were shown to our quarters in Rundale Castle. We had to sleep on the floor in the downstairs corridors and were forbidden to go into the rooms above as they still retained some of their former splendour. An intensive programme of physical exercises started immediately to prepare us for our return to the front line.

At first the discipline seemed unnecessarily strict for experienced soldiers. Perhaps we were considered to have become soft during our life in hospital and to have lost all our respect for authority. As a punishment for slovenly behaviour many of us had to wade across the pond in the castle grounds and climb the ornamental fountain in its middle. We also had realistic battle training in the coastal meadows by the River Lielupe, and carried out landing exercises with rubber boats in the same river. There were accidents when the defenders on the 'enemy' bank shot some of those landing from close range as live ammunition was being used.

As midsummer's night approached we prepared to celebrate in the usual Latvian manner. We had got together plenty to eat and drink and hired a band of musicians – the only thing missing was the traditional St John's Night fires. Russian aircraft had been seen recently in Lithuania and we were strictly forbidden to show any light at all. But this did not worry anyone. The band assembled on the castle balcony and played without stopping. Girls from the surrounding countryside had brought with them the usual St John's Night wreaths which they placed on the heads of the Legionnaires, and everyone danced around the fountain in the castle forecourt. By early morning the yard was empty. Many had become overcome by drink and had gone to sleep, while others had gone for long walks in the park with the girls. Unfortunately I could not take part in the celebrations. The previous evening I had been ordered to be the company duty NCO and had to spend the whole night in the castle looking after the company's quarters.

I stayed at Rundale for another week and then we were told that we would be returning to the front line. Only those of us who were still in poor shape and unfit for duty were left behind. The rest of us boarded the narrow-gauge train one afternoon and went to Meitene where we transferred to another train which would take us all the way to the Eastern Front.

We left Meitene late that night. Most of the men went to sleep while a few sat up around a candle in one corner of the wagon. They were card players and preferred not to sleep. It began to rain and was still raining when we reached Jelgava where we stopped for a couple of hours.

When we began to wake up Jelgava was far behind us. On opening the wagon doors we could see extensive forests and marshland in the grey morning light. We were heading for Krustpils and not Riga as we had hoped. After a short stop at Krustpils the train continued on its way.

As it was a hot day some of us had climbed onto the roof of the wagon to escape the heat. We were dressed only in swimming trunks – just like at the seaside. For hour after hour the train continued its journey. Quite often we had to lie down to escape being swept off the roof by low bridges and telegraph wires. We would have preferred to have returned to the inside of the wagon but this would have been risky while the train was in motion. It became cold with the setting of the sun and we were glad to get off the roof at Varaklani when the train stopped there. We reached Rezekne the same evening and spent the night there.

The next morning we went for a swim in the sandy bottomed

river and then were each given a bowl of soup from the soldiers' kitchen. Continuing on our way all afternoon we crossed the Russian border the next night. There were watchtowers manned by railway guards alongside the line now and we also saw some wagons and locomotives which had been blown up by the partisans and were lying on their sides in the ditches on both sides of the railway line.

All the next day we continued our journey through Russia. While the train was standing at a station in the afternoon there were excited shouts to take cover and at the same time the anti-aircraft guns on the train opened fire. It was already too late to find proper cover. Cannon and machine-gun fire was already exploding smacking into the ground all around us. The only possible cover was in some shallow ditches in the fields near the railway line, but these did not offer much protection. The Russian planes had attacked from the direction of the sun and had surprised our air sentries. After the first attack the planes turned back to try their luck once more, but this time our anti-aircraft gunners were ready for them and the concentrated fire from the train's guns forced them to turn away and they disappeared to the east.

We had not got away without loss. A dead soldier was carried out from the next wagon to mine, hit by machine-gun bullets from the air before he could reach the front line. Near the station a large barn full of hay was ablaze and this had set fire to the ammunition wagon. As long as this wagon was burning the exploding ammunition prevented anyone from approaching it to try and put the fire out. We had to wait until the fire had burnt out before we could continue our journey.

We reached Opochka as the sun set and immediately set off on foot for the front line. I had met an old friend on the train, Corporal Andermanis, who I had known in the Guards Company. During that first night's march we were ordered to go ahead of the main column of marching men to protect them from surprise attack by partisans.

In the quiet summer's night we walked as carefully as any Indian scouts towards the south where there was a bridge across the river to our left, but we met no one on the road that night. We could see the far-off glow of flares and hear the distant rumble of gunfire in the direction of the front line. We had to search every bush at the side of the road, a nerve-racking business. Our eyes were constantly staring into the darkness as we knew only too well that our chances of survival depended on us seeing the enemy first, and yet we felt a strange sense of adventure. We were ready for instant action. The other men in our scouting patrol followed us a short distance behind and then came the main body of the column. They too had spread out along both sides of the road in single file and had their rifles at the ready.

We had only a couple of short rest breaks during that night and were able to speed up when it became light as we did not have to be so wary of partisans any more. When we reached the bridge we turned off the main highway towards the east, crossed the river and dispersed in the woods on the left side of the road where we were told we could rest all day. We slept on the ground in the shade of the trees along the river bank until Russian aircraft attacked the bridge in the afternoon with machine guns and cannon. We did not go to view the damage afterwards but could hear shouting coming from the direction of the bridge – it seemed that the bridge had been hit.

Leaving the river after dark that evening, we continued on our way. The road was quite new, consisting of wooden blocks and built by the Germans to serve the front line. We walked along each side of the road in single file. Everything was very quiet and the few lorries and carts were soon swallowed up in the darkness and rising clouds of dust after they had passed us. An attack by Russian aircraft was taking place a couple of miles ahead of us. We could see the flares and ascending tracer from our anti-aircraft guns. Later on, passing the place where the attack had taken place, we saw the bomb craters in the fields on both sides of the road. In the windless night the smoke and smell of explosives had not yet dispersed, but hung over the ground like thin clouds of morning mist. It seemed that this time the Russians had missed their target completely.

The sun was just rising when we stopped to rest for the day on the banks of another river – the Alolja. The small bridge was already prepared for blowing up by the Germans in case of a Russian breakthrough. They had placed two large aerial bombs on both sides of the bridge which were guarded by two German soldiers. We rested peacefully all day in some lakeside bushes, continued our march the next night and reached our destination, the village of Krasnoje, early in the morning. We were split up here according to our units and then sent on to the various regimental headquarters. My friend the Corporal was given command of my group and, led by him, we went to the headquarters of the 32nd Regiment in Lavi.

The bunkers here were substantially built and well camouflaged by the forest on the left side of the road. We were lined up in the shade of the trees, inspected and greeted by the new commander of the Regiment, Aperats. We heard rumours that the former commander, Kripens, had been dismissed from his job for the inefficient fulfilment of his duties during the St John's Day battle. We did not know how much of this was true but on the whole were well pleased with our new commander, whose appearance inspired confidence. Later on, on the way to the front-line trenches, our guide pointed out to us the so-called St John's Hill and told us about the many attacks and counter-attacks, and of the many men who had fallen on the night of our national festival.

Very soon we were approaching the front line. We saw a sign at the roadside written in Latvian: 'ARTILLERY FIRE ZONE – HELMETS MUST BE WORN FROM HERE.' We entered a birch forest which was criss-crossed with communication trenches, the trunks of the trees mutilated by shell splinters; we could clearly see the shallow craters left by the impact of enemy mortar bombs.

The Company Commander was a complete stranger to me, nor did I recognize any of the soldiers near his bunker when we reported there. At first the commander wanted to split us up and divide us among his platoons, but then changed his mind. We were to remain under his direct command for special duties. He appointed my friend the Corporal to command the Company Headquarters and I was made Number One on the machine gun. We had to stay in a bunker quite close to the headquarters. When the previous occupants had vacated the bunker they had christened it by leaving an inscription over the door: 'THE PARISH COUNCIL HOUSE OF PURMALE.' By night we posted a sentry with a machine gun near the bunker's entrance, while the rest of us slept peacefully inside. The machine-gun position had been excellently constructed, making it possible to fire in any direction. A short communications trench led directly to the Company Commander's bunker.

*   *   *

We spent two or three peaceful days here, visited our friends in the front line, got to know about life there and told them about our experiences in hospital. Very few of our friends were left and they were glad to see us. We mentioned some names and received the same reply: dead, missing, wounded. We could only tell them about those we had met during our stay at various hospitals – about the fate of others we could only guess.

One day we visited the strongpoint on the extreme left of our company's front-line sector, following rumours that one of our mates from the Guards Company commanded a section there. Before reaching the strongpoint the birch forest ended and to continue on our way we had to jump into a trench to cross an open field. The strongpoint itself had been built into the top of a small hill and from there we could see for some distance all around. We saw the narrow gap of land between two lakes, the trenches of our neighbouring regiment, the Russian trenches and their rear area. We were told to be extra careful when observing over the parapet during daytime. The Russians had precisely ranged one of their quick-firing anti-tank guns on this position and whenever they saw movement they opened fire.

On 9 July we heard a semi-official rumour that we were going to withdraw to a new front line the next day. In order to be prepared for any eventuality, I thoroughly cleaned and oiled my machine gun, then went to the front-line trenches to try it out. The trenches here followed the edge of a forest from which I could see the Russian line approximately 400 yards away. I fired off a whole belt of ammunition into the Russian trenches while my friend the Corporal observed the fall of shot through his binoculars. The gun worked faultlessly and my aim was good. As soon as we had finished the test firing we disappeared into a nearby bunker following the advice of the soldiers stationed there. We were just in time – Russian mortar bombs started to explode all around us almost immediately and when we finally emerged we saw that one of the entrance posts had been shattered by a direct hit.

That afternoon I refilled the empty belt with ammunition and prepared for the march the next day. As it became dark we could see the blaze of numerous fires to the west. Villages to the rear of the front line were already burning and we did not like the look of it at all. Such fires told the Russians that we were preparing to withdraw and we did not think that they would let us get away in peace. In the quiet of the night we could hear the sound of numerous engines from the direction of the Russian lines. We could also hear shouting and singing, which indicated that they were preparing to move as well.

A group of men approached our trenches from the rear, crossed the front line and disappeared quietly into no-man's-land. This was a mine-laying party whose job was to surprise the Russians if they tried to approach us without due care. On the whole, the night passed quietly with only the occasional rifle shot and a mortar bomb which exploded some distance from us.

We had already set up the machine gun outside the bunker and were preparing to go to sleep when a runner arrived from the Company Commander. He ordered us all to get dressed and report to Company's Headquarters without delay. There we were told to go to the trenches of our neighbouring battalion to investigate the situation. Unconfirmed reports had reached our Company Headquarters of a Russian breakthrough and we were to find out if this was true.

Approaching the front line from the rear we came to the headquarters of the neighbouring company, but could not find out anything to clarify things. They knew roughly where the Russians had broken into the front line and sent one of their men with us as a guide. We neared the trenches cautiously and as we got close we could hear someone speaking in Latvian so knew that the enemy were no longer there. We got to know that a group of Russians had crossed the front line having come up so quietly that the sentry had only noticed them when they leaped over the trench. He had shot at them but the Russians had disappeared into the bushes to the rear of our line. Now our neighbours had no idea where the Russians were or what they were doing. They were no longer in the immediate area of the front line – that much they did know.

We decided to stay with our neighbours for the rest of the night to help out in case of any trouble. The rest of the night was spent watching and listening for any sign of the enemy until at first light we were able to view the country around us. There was a clearing in the forest between us and the Russians, and in the middle of this was a small log cabin. To find out if there were any Russians inside we shot it up with our machine guns. The wooden walls splintered but we could not see any sign of life. We could safely assume that there were no live enemy in the cabin because we knew that the bullets had passed right through it. By this time the sun had risen, everything was peaceful and we returned to our company.

Chapter 14

The Retreat from Russia, 10–15 July 1944

10 July 1944

We reported to the Company Commander and he sent us to our bunker to get some sleep before the retreat that evening. As I was not feeling too tired I wrote a letter before turning in. In the event I did not have much time to sleep for someone from outside suddenly wrenched open the door with such force that we all sat up as the runner shouted, 'Stand to! A Russian attack is imminent!' As if to reinforce this we could hear heavy shelling outside which made us jump up, grab our weapons and equipment, and run out of the bunker. Outside we could hear that the shells were not falling in our immediate vicinity but on the trenches to the north of us. A few mortar bombs were landing near us but the right wing of the neighbouring 33rd Regiment was receiving a real pasting. We could only wait and see. We would be in a difficult position if the Russians decided to start a major offensive, as we were preparing to withdraw that evening and our artillery had already pulled back.

The Russian gunfire continued for about half an hour and then by the sound of it the Russian infantry was starting to assault our neighbours. As the bombardment ended, it became quieter and I could clearly hear the voice of our Company Commander shouting in an agitated voice, 'Whatever you do don't let the Russians get through the gap between the lakes. If they do everything's lost.' I had no idea who he was talking to – he may have been telephoning

101

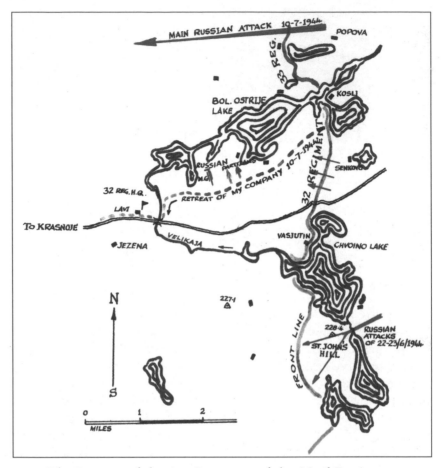

The Retreat of the 1st Company of the 32nd Regiment.
10 July 1944.

the 33rd Regiment but it was possible that he was giving instructions to the strongpoint on our extreme left wing. This strongpoint was situated in front of our trenches and their machine guns covered the gap between the lakes. If it was the latter then his order was already too late. Very soon a runner arrived from this strongpoint and reported to the commander that they had a lot of casualties and wounded. The Russians had broken through the neighbouring regiment after a very heavy bombardment by enemy artillery and mortars, which had been so concentrated that the trenches had caved in. Our men in the strongpoint had come under accurate fire from enemy anti-tank guns which prevented them from using their machine guns. Soon they neither dared show themselves nor use their weapons.

The runner was very frightened. His hands were shaking and he accidentally fired the Very pistol hanging from his belt. The flare did not go up in the air but hit the top of his boot and before he could get it off he was severely burnt on his left leg. After he had been bandaged the runner departed limping to the rear.

Meanwhile Russian artillery fire on us increased, their shells landing in the birch forest, mutilating the tree trunks with their splinters, breaking off branches and throwing up fountains of earth. We expected the Russians to attack us at any moment and were prepared for it. We stood to with our rifles and machine guns, and made ready the hand grenades piled up on the sides of the trench.

At last it was time to pull out. The Company Commander appeared from the bunker where he had been sheltering up until then, communicating with the outside world by telephone. We were ordered to cover the retreat of the rest of the company through the lakeside forest. We passed a group of Legionnaires pulling an anti-tank gun and went down the hill towards open fields.

As we emerged from the forest we could clearly see the whole company in front of us. We could also see another column of soldiers descending the low hills to the rear of our former front line, but at that distance it was impossible to distinguish whether they were our men or the enemy.[1]

It was a hot day and sweat ran down our backs when we crossed the open space carrying our heavy equipment. All of a sudden we were fired on by rifles, light machine guns fired from the woods to our right, and we could clearly see the tracer passing over the heads of the men in the Company. For a moment there was some confusion but then the Company Commander raised his hand and pointed to the woods. As one man the company turned and after a short dash reached the edge of the forest. As soon as I reached the trees I threw myself down and started firing my machine gun, but as I could not pick out a target among the thick birch trees, I stopped after a few short bursts. Our fire was not returned and gradually the company ceased firing. It seemed that our sharp, decisive action had beaten off our attackers and they had run away. We had no time to search the forest so pulled back to the field, formed up into platoons and continued on our way.

The forest to our right soon ended and the Company was dropping down into a shallow depression when, without warning, we came under machine-gun fire from the right. The fire was so well aimed and delivered from such close quarters that terrible confusion arose in the ranks of the Company. The Company Commander fell with his arm raised to order another counter-attack. Within minutes many of his men had been killed and the rest of them dispersed to seek some form of shelter from the hail of bullets. But there was little cover in the field and the Russian machine gun continued its deadly work.

When our group at last emerged from the protective cover of the forest we came across a terrible sight – our dead and wounded lay all over the shallow marshy depression in the ground. Some of the wounded were trying to crawl towards the cover of a nearby rye field, but they were stopped by Russian fire. Their machine gun was clearly visible on a low hill to the right of the hollow only a couple of hundred yards from us. The machine gun kept up a steady fire and I could see some Russians near it shouting at our men to surrender. The Russian machine gunners had not noticed our group emerging from the shade of the birch forest and our only chance of escaping capture was to cross the depression into the woods on the other side. I quickly lay on the ground, took careful aim on the Russian machine-gun crew and pulled the trigger. Nothing happened! I tried to pull back the bolt to eject the faulty cartridge, but it had jammed and would not shift. I tried to open the lid on top of the weapon but without success. The gun was useless and all I could do was rely on my legs to carry me through as we ran across the depression. Meanwhile the Russians had spotted us and their bullets were whizzing all around us. The enemy fire quietened down a bit when my friend the Corporal opened fire on them with his machine pistol from behind me. I tried to get across the patch of marshy ground in the middle of the hollow as quickly as possible, but I was hindered by my great skiing boots and the weight of the machine gun. The Corporal caught up with me and shouted, 'Do not mess about! Throw the bone saw away and get into the rye!'[2] He had expended all his ammunition and the Russians had begun firing once more. I tossed the useless gun as far as I could into the marsh and together with the Corporal reached the field of rye. We crawled through the corn towards the woods followed by Russian bullets, reached the edge of the field and disappeared into the forest.[3]

A small group of us assembled near the edge of the woods: all that was left of our company. We tossed a few hand grenades into the bushes at the lakeside to scare the Russians off, and then started to walk quickly through the forest towards the west, badly shaken by our recent experience. We did not know if we were already completely surrounded by the enemy and we had only a few weapons left. I had a couple of hand grenades stuck into my belt and another which I carried in my hand ready to throw.

After passing through the forest we came to the bridge over the small River Velikaja near the headquarters of the 32nd Regiment. We were commanded by Corporal Andermanis who was the most senior among us now.

On the other side of the river we met a couple of observers hiding in the bushes and watching for the approach of the enemy. The headquarters was already abandoned and the bunkers burnt out or blown up. There was no officer in sight and after telling the two men about the fate of our company we continued on our way to the rear.

We spent all the afternoon on the road and it was already dark when we reached the village of Krasnoje where there was a long column of soldiers passing through, withdrawing to the west. A house was burning somewhere in the village lighting up the road which passed close to a stone wall on the left-hand side. This wall was constantly struck by bullets which came from somewhere on the right of the road. The enemy had already got this far!

To get past the wall we walked in the ditches on both sides of the road as the bullets cracked harmlessly over our heads. Any vehicles had to be driven as fast as possible through the hail of bullets.

Behind the village of Krasnoje we were stopped by an officer who practically begged us to go and check over a clump of trees about 500 yards to the right of the road. If necessary he would cover us with fire from the anti-aircraft guns which he had lined up on the road, their barrels pointing towards the north. However, on closer inspection, the officer noticed that we had few weapons and were in a bad state, so decided otherwise. 'Go to the rear, boys,' he said, 'but try to get your hands on some weapons somewhere, otherwise you'll be in trouble!'

We did not have to be told twice. As soon as we had started walking along the road again several artillery shells landed in the village. We could also hear shouting from the clump of trees which the officer had wanted us to look at which meant that the Russians were there already. A large piece of shrapnel flew low over our heads and fell on the road raising a cloud of dust. We crouched down and quickened our pace to try and put some distance between ourselves and the village as soon as possible. We walked in this way all night.

11 July 1944

We neared the village of Panowo as the sun rose after a night spent on the road. We had got to know that the Supply Unit of our company was there and after a short search we found them. The Supply men received us as someone returning from the dead. They had heard about the fate of our Company and were delighted to see us, although they were very sympathetic when we told them about the events of the previous day.

They had supplies for the whole company and because it had almost ceased to exist any more we were allowed to take anything we wanted. We also received a couple of bottles of vodka which the Supply men had somehow 'organized' during the night. Any of us in need of a weapon was given a rifle and ammunition. We stuffed a few hand grenades into our belts and our spirits improved. We were once again ready to defend ourselves against any eventuality.

The CO of the Supply Unit could not let us stay there for long as he had just received orders to send everyone back along the road leading to the north, out of the village and to a new blocking position which was being created to stop the Russian advance. We were each given another mug of hot coffee and then set off along the road indicated. When the village was a couple of hundred yards behind us we left the road for a meal and a rest. We were hungry after the all-night night march and we had a drink as well. With the first bottle empty and the second being passed round from hand to hand, we noticed a car approaching along the road. It stopped near us and some officers got out, one of whom shouted in German, calling us over to him. We ran to the car and a high-ranking officer immediately asked Corporal Andermanis who we were and what we were doing. The Corporal did not know much German and although he tried to explain he did not get anywhere. We were in trouble and the officer was getting more and more impatient. In the end the Corporal pointed to me and said 'Dolmetcher'.[4] My time with the Guards Company now stood me in good stead. I clicked my heels, saluted according to regulations and reported, giving the name of our unit and our destination. More importantly, I addressed the officer by his correct rank. When he asked me the whereabouts of our company I told him what had happened the day before. I also told him that we were only resting for a short time before continuing on our way to the front line. The officer became more amenable. 'Good,' he said, 'you at least have weapons – do not stay here for long but get going!'[5]

We did not dare rest any longer but picked up our weapons and equipment and started on our way. We did not have to go far – perhaps a mile or so. Here the countryside to the east of the road was open, with a low, marshy, wooded area on the other side to the west. Further west we could see a lake overgrown with reeds. The road north continued for another half mile and then turned sharply out of sight to the east. There was some rising ground a couple of hundred yards to the east of the road and on it we could see a line of Legionnaires in position. We were assigned to another company, which for the moment was assembled in the field between the road and the hill, to be instructed in the use of anti-tank projectiles, or 'Panzerfausts', a weapon which we were seeing for the first time. The instructor, a young Lieutenant, had just arrived from the front. His smoke-grimed face had a couple of days' growth of beard on it, but he knew his job. He explained quickly and simply the aiming and firing of the projectile and demonstrated by firing off a couple of the new rockets.

All this clearly indicated the imminence of a tank attack, and the constant flow of lorries and carts at high speed along the road to the rear made it plain that they were probably not far away. Some of the drivers were riding on horses, drinking straight from bottles of vodka and shouting to us, 'The tanks are coming!'

When the stream of vehicles and carts ended and the dust clouds rising from their wheels had subsided, we could hear somewhere to our front the sound of powerful engines and the clatter of caterpillar tracks. We could also hear the sharp cracks of tank guns and the rattle of machine guns. Some of the Legionnaires panicked, left their positions on the hill and tried to run back, but they were stopped by their officers with drawn revolvers and returned to the position.

My friend the Corporal and I picked up a couple of the new anti-tank rockets and camouflaged ourselves in position on the left-hand side of the road where we were well covered by the bushes. We were excited but tried to keep calm so that we would not miss the tanks with our new weapons. We knew that a decisive moment was at hand. Some of the other Legionnaires joined us and spread out in the undergrowth near the road. We checked our rear for an escape route in case our efforts to stop the tanks were in vain. The marshy ground did not look too promising but at least there would be ample cover in the bushes. We knew that we would not be able to retreat to the village because the road would be covered by fire from the tanks.

We spent an anxious hour expecting Russian tanks to appear at any moment, but when it became quiet in front of us we were told that they had been stopped. We were relieved and lay down at the roadside resting and smoking.

The afternoon passed and it was early evening when we were ordered to prepare to leave. We handed over the Panzerfausts to the Supply men who were to transport them on their wagons and started on the road back to Panowo. We could hear explosions to the east where the road from Krasnoje entered the village. The earth shook and great columns of smoke shot up in the air. The Germans were blowing up the road to stop the enemy from following us. In Panowo we passed a dead Latvian Legionnaire lying face down in one of the roadside ditches. We could not imagine what had happened to him and only later realized his probable fate – he was probably one of the deserters the Divisional Commander had shot earlier that day.

After passing through the village we turned onto the road to the west and very soon entered a large forest. We could still hear explosions going on behind us, but with the approach of darkness they ended and all became quiet. A couple of hours later, as we entered a part of the forest that was completely burnt out, we overtook an artillery unit. The heavy guns had got bogged down in the sandy road surface and we had to help them to get going on their way to the rear. Having assisted the artillery we continued westwards on our weary way through the warm night, heading towards where we were supposed to occupy a new front line.

12 July 1944

By now it was becoming light. Although the sun had risen we could not see it as we were enveloped in smoke from the forest, which was still burning, together with morning mist. The destruction of the endless forest was attributed to the Germans who had apparently burnt it down in order to deny the partisans access to the road. A pall of smoke hung over the entire countryside and the fate of this particular forest made us think that the same could soon happen in our own country.[6]

We were tired. We had spent all night on the road and we hoped to have put enough ground between us and the enemy to be able to rest for at least à day. As the morning mist cleared with the rising sun, we left the forest. On entering open country we could see quite a long way and someone soon noticed something unusual – a tall, wooden, fire-watching tower a couple of miles from us that already carried the red flag. Had the Russians advanced this far? The question was on everybody's lips. A group of German soldiers at the roadside did not think so. They told us that the flag must be the work of partisans and that the enemy's forces were still some distance away.

Having walked along the road for another hour we were finally allowed to leave it and rest on the steep embankment. To the right of us the country was flat and open, and we scoured it for any sign of the enemy. Everything seemed peaceful and quiet. The sun was already well up, it was becoming hot and the heat haze shimmered over the fields and meadows. As we waited for further orders, some men had already gone to sleep.

The sleepers were woken by the sound of approaching aircraft and sat up while the rest of us tried to identify the direction from which they were coming. And then we saw them – three aircraft flying towards us from the direction of the burnt-out forest. They were keeping low, with the sun behind them, and we could not distinguish whether they were Russian or German. To be on the safe side we took cover in the roadside ditches and it was only when they were overhead that we could see the red stars on their wings. The aircraft were so low that we could see the faces of the pilots in

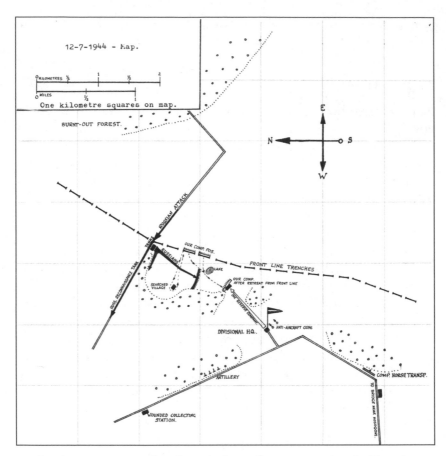

Explanatory map for description of retreat action in Russia,
12 July 1944. Drawn from memory in 1962 and not to be
considered as accurate in detail.

the cockpits, but they did not open fire or drop any bombs – it seemed that these were Russian reconnaissance planes. After flying over us they gained height, turned and disappeared towards the east.

A short while later we received orders to move, but this time we did not have to go far. We passed through a line of trenches before being split up and shown the length of front line we were to occupy. The trenches were well constructed along a line of low hills, with strongpoints forward of them. All the trees and bushes in front of the line had been cut down leaving foot-high stumps which were enmeshed in barbed wire. We were especially pleased with the bunkers which were deep underground, each of them with two entrance stairways. They were reinforced overhead with several layers of crossed timber and were so well camouflaged that they were undetectable above ground. They were quite level and blended in to the hillside perfectly.[7]

It seemed that the Germans had spent a long time preparing the new line and intended to hold it, but to do so we needed more men. Over the last couple of days our companies had been reduced to about twenty men each and we had lost most of our weapons at the same time. The company commanders busied themselves in the trenches trying to deploy their men as effectively as possible in the long sectors assigned to them. Some of the men were given the task of digging a communication trench from the bunker to the machine-gun position in the front line but I, with a group of Legionnaires, was given another task.

While the front line was being made ready for battle we had to secure the rear of it by evicting the occupants of a village about a mile behind it. We knew that such a seemingly simple task could turn out to be a bloody battle if we met any partisans and so approached the village with caution. After watching it for a while we could not make out any sign of life – the dozen or so houses seemed deserted and after running across the fields we reached the first house. One of us kicked the door open while the rest covered him with our rifles. We searched the house and then went to the next one, but they were both empty. Eventually we found the village inhabitants, about ten of them, hiding in one room. Leaving one man to guard them we searched the rest of the village but did not find anyone else. We returned to the villagers and one man who could speak Russian ordered them to leave at once in the direction of Opochka. The Russians did not want to go. They told us that they themselves had only just arrived here fleeing from the Russians, and they wanted to rest for a couple of days before continuing their journey. The men were especially argumentative, but we did not have time to explain why they had to leave at once. We ended the argument by pointing our guns threateningly at them and they gathered their belongings before walking off across the fields towards Opochka.

We were now free to search the village for anything useful. Some chickens were scratching around near one of the houses and some of the Legionnaires started chasing them but failed to catch any as the hens disappeared under the buildings. Others had better luck when they found a pig rooting in one of the fields and killed the animal. We carried the pig back to the trenches, together with a large cauldron to cook it in, and were greeted by a great cheer when we arrived there.

After a while I changed into swimming trunks and joined in the digging of the communication trench. Others were busy butchering the pig ready for cooking, but we were not allowed to finish either of these jobs.

Around three o'clock in the afternoon a couple of shells exploded in no-man's-land, throwing up fountains of earth and smoke. We assumed that this was our artillery firing some ranging rounds and continued our work in the sun. The next shell fell close to the trenches and it became clear that it was the Russians who were ranging onto us. We left the digging and went into the bunker to put on our uniforms. On the way we had to take cover several times to avoid the bullets fired from an enemy aircraft which had suddenly appeared overhead. Having quickly got dressed we reloaded our rifles and climbed up the bunker stairs to the trench.

Above ground we were greeted by the sound of battle coming from the left. We could hear shouts, the firing of automatic weapons and the clatter of tank tracks in the direction of a village about a mile to the north of us. A line of Legionnaires emerged from the village, took cover in some ditches and began to fire at the houses. A Russian tank followed them along the tree-lined road and moved off quickly towards our rear. Firing near the village increased and the Legionnaires were gradually retreating towards us so that we were in real danger of being attacked from two sides. We had been under increasing artillery fire for some time and could expect a frontal attack at any minute – now we were threatened from the rear as well. We were too few to offer any real resistance, but at the same time our CO did not want to take the responsibility of giving the order to retreat. All communications with the Regiment and Division were cut or had not yet been established.

We watched the progress of the battle in the neighbouring village for about another quarter of an hour. Suddenly the Legionnaires left their line of defence and were immediately followed by a thick line of Russians in two groups, one chasing the Legionnaires who had abandoned the village and the other heading straight for us. The time had come for a decision – whether to stand and fight without much chance of survival, or to pull out from our positions. Our commander decided on the latter course. We jumped out of the trenches and disappeared into dead ground running off in the direction of another village to the rear of the front line. At that time the enemy were still about 300 yards from us and the village to which we were retreating was some distance off. The sun was very hot, we were sweating and thirsty, and on the way nearly everybody had a drink from a small, peaceful lake enclosed by trees and bushes.

The village had been built on a low hill and from it we could clearly see the long line of Russians following us. It was an excellent defensive position and we opened effective fire along the fence on the edge of the village. 'Just like being on the rifle range,' we shouted to each other. The Russians were plainly visible in the afternoon sun and they had very little cover in the ploughed fields. Many of them fell and remained lying there, while the rest took up positions in ditches and were very soon firing back at us. But their aim was poor as they were facing directly into the sun and could not see us in the shadows cast by the village trees. We were worried about our left flank where the enemy were still advancing, but they too were very soon stopped by the familiar sound of German machine guns which we could hear from that direction, and we knew we were not alone.

A short while later we also heard rifle and machine-gun fire from behind us, a new development which we did not like at all. If they were Russians we were surrounded and in serious trouble. I called a couple of my comrades and we went to clarify the situation to the rear of the village. We crouched behind the end houses of the village from where we could see that we were safe. A whole company or more of Legionnaires were approaching our village spread out in a line across the fields and their machine gunners were firing on our positions. The situation was critical. We could not show ourselves as the machine-gun bullets were smacking into the houses with monotonous regularity. It was obvious that they thought that the village was already in Russian hands. Someone tied a handkerchief on the bayonet of his rifle and waved it around a corner; I did the same with my steel helmet and the firing ceased. Only then did we leave our cover, shouting to them to stop firing and waving our arms. We were just in time. The company was only a hundred yards away, their rifles were at the ready and they were on the point of rushing the village.

We were immediately asked all sorts of questions, then two officers appeared and I reported the situation to one of them. We went back into the village without further delay and the newcomers spread out among our men in the firing line.

During my absence my friend the Corporal had disappeared – I was told that he had been wounded and taken to the centre of the village. After a short search I found him in one of the houses. The bullet had passed through his left side and his face was grey from pain and loss of blood. 'Don't leave me to the Russians,' he kept repeating and I told him I would see to it that he was taken to the rear. I ran back to the firing line and ordered three men to come with me. We improvised a stretcher from rifles and groundsheets and started to carry the Corporal to the next village where the temporary Divisional Headquarters of the Latvian Legion was situated.[8] The Corporal was a big man. Very soon we were sweating profusely and our arms and legs ached, but we continued on our way with short rests every now and then. We had about half a mile to go, and when we reached the village we found a doctor there but no transport for the wounded. There were a lot of high-ranking officers there and they asked us about the situation in our village; one of them observed it through tripod-mounted binoculars. Several anti-tank guns, well camouflaged in the orchards and bushes, were pointing towards the enemy ready to fire at a moment's notice.

The Corporal had bled a lot while we were carrying him and a pool of blood had gathered in the groundsheet when we lifted him up from it. Having sent the other men back to the front line I took advantage of the confusion in Divisional Headquarters and remained with the Corporal. Half an hour later an ammunitions wagon took my friend to the rear and I went with him. We parted at the casualty collecting station a couple of miles further back. The corporal thanked me by shaking my hand but said nothing – his face was pale and he was in great pain.[9]

I went back to Divisional Headquarters alone. It was already dark. A battery of our field guns had taken up a position at the roadside. They were camouflaged in the thick bushes and fired non-

Front row: my two sisters and I; back row: my grandfather flanked by my great-aunts.

ool summer camp. I am third from the right in the back row (marked with an X).

The street in Riga where my mother lived from 1938 to 1974.

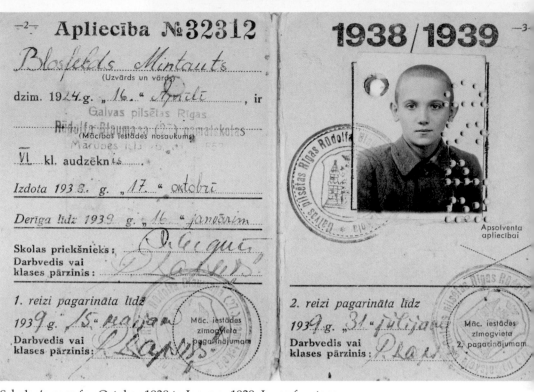

Scholar's pass for October 1938 to January 1939. I was fourteen.

Identity card for January 1943, just before I was called up.

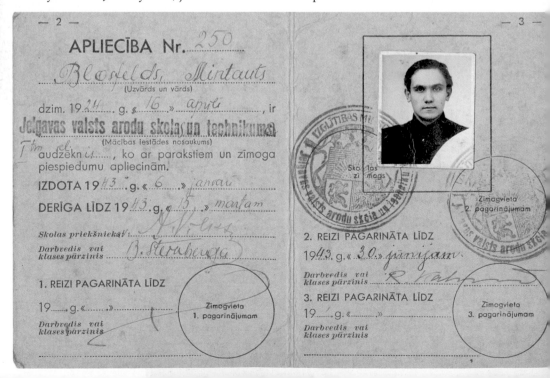

My cousin Andulis (right)
and I in Waffen SS uniform.

The beginning: recruits of the Latvian Legion
marching. Paplaka, Summer 1943.

The Generalinspektor
of the Latvian Legion,
General R. Bangerskis,
inspecting the Guards
Company, Riga,
Summer 1943.
I am in the front rank,
7th from the right.

One of the inns in Kreutzberg, near Bad Johannisbrunn, Czechoslovakia.

The inn where I spent my Christmas leave in 1944. Kreutzberg, near Bad Johannisbrunn, Czechoslova

...ction: the fighting in Russia. Summer, 1944.

... end: the barracks in Zedelghem Prisoner-of-War Camp 2227. Autumn, 1945.

Gate from Cage 2 to
Cage 1, Zedelghem.

Roll call, Zedelghem.

Announcing our release,
Zedelghem.

Doncaster, 1949.

Iris and I on our
wedding day,
21 July 1951.

On a hiking holiday, 1977.

Wedding anniversary
while on holiday, 1986.

stop, covered by thick clouds of smoke from the guns which did not drift away but hung around them like morning mist. On reaching Divisional Headquarters I could see that our anti-aircraft guns were also firing on the enemy. Their tracer flew in long arcs between the villages towards the Russians who had still not managed to take our village.

I did not feel like returning to the front line at night as I was tired from three days and nights without proper sleep or rest and decided to go to the Supply Unit of our company for a good night's sleep. I had discovered that the unit was quartered a couple of miles further back and continued on my way there along the dark road.

I knew the commander of the Supply Unit from my Guards Company days. He greeted me warmly and said that he could make use of me. They had been strafed and bombed by Russian aircraft, and the next day they had to move. I could take the place of one of the wounded drivers. At first I did not fancy the idea, but he decided the matter for me. 'Don't be stupid. This'll give you a chance to take things easy.' I was in two minds about his offer – I was tempted to accept it, but also felt it was my duty to return to my own unit in the front line. In the end I decided to stay where I was at least until the morning and then make a decision.

We had some supper, attended to the horses and went to sleep in the wagons using horse blankets to cover us. By that time the front line had quietened down. We were occasionally disturbed by Russian aircraft flying slowly overhead, but at least they did not drop any bombs near us, limiting their attacks to the roads further back where we could see their flares descending slowly prior to their bombing runs.

13 July 1944

We were awakened by the sound of battle nearby and could hear the rattle of rifles and machine guns, and the explosions of mortar bombs, coming from behind the forest in which we had spent the night. Sometimes we could also hear the firing of a 'Stalin Organ' – the famous Russian multi-barrelled rocket launcher – and the drumming of the explosions.

We had slept a long time. The sun was already well up, the air was hot and close but we were protected to some extent by the shade of the trees. Someone decided we should search the forest to the immediate rear of the front line for partisans, to prevent an attack from that direction. A long line of Legionnaires emerged from the village, turned to the right and disappeared into the forest with their rifles at the ready. The fire from the forest continued unabated as Russian rockets kept on coming and the village caught fire. The flames soon spread from one straw-covered roof to another and soon the whole village was ablaze. All around was confusion.

We were given an order to leave at once, drive to the bridge and after crossing the river to continue to Opochka. We had already packed everything onto the wagons, harnessed the horses and were able to set off immediately.

While passing the burning village we met a platoon of Legionnaires advancing towards the front line, led by the commander of the 32nd Latvian Regiment, Aperats. His greying head was bare and he had rolled up the sleeves of his shirt. He carried a machine pistol and shouted to his soldiers, 'Lets go, lads, and show the Ivans what we Latvians can do!' The Legionnaires followed him without hesitation and disappeared behind the smoke and flames of the burning village, while we went the other way, to the rear, the bridge and safety.

The country here was hilly but open. Just before the bridge there was a long curve in the road which was jammed with army transport. No one was attempting to cross the bridge which was enveloped with smoke from Russian shells that were falling all round it. As we waited for the fire to slacken we were helped by a sudden thunderstorm. It rained so heavily that we were wet through in no time but did not mind at all as the rain also prevented Russian artillery observers from seeing the bridge and adjusting their fire. With the shells exploding wide of their target, we started to move to cross the bridge while hidden from the enemy by the curtain of rain.

When our turn came we drove the horses at a quick trot across the wooden bridge while we ourselves ran beside the wagons. Although the current below the bridge seemed ominously fast as the river was in spate, it was not very wide and we were soon across. Even as we reached other side a shell exploded by the road, throwing up a great cloud of sand and smoke. The horses strained and pulled the wagons quickly up the steep incline, and as the rain died away we reached the main road to the north and Opochka.

After continuing for another hour we eventually left the road for a rest until the evening, drying our clothes and boots in the sun and feeding the horses.

Setting off again in the gathering gloom, we approached Opochka when it was quite dark. Our artillery had taken up positions near the southern outskirts of the town and were firing non-stop at the enemy, which frightened our horses. In front of us the sky was lit up by the burning town and behind us we could see the glimmer of front-line flares. We drove into the town and were directed by the German military police to turn to the left, towards the border of Latvia. Leaving the burning town behind us we continued in the dark along the road which was jammed by military transport. As we wanted to put as much distance as possible between us and the Russians, we carried on slowly until the morning and only then stopped to rest the horses and get some sleep ourselves.

14 July 1944

We spent the day resting in a small copse at the roadside. The road from Opochka to Latvia was crammed with traffic but was saved from Russian air attacks by the thick fog which persisted all day. At times the road was so jammed with wagons and lorries that they had to stand motionless for hours and would have offered an easy target for Russian aircraft if they had not been hidden by the fog.

15 July 1944

It was already getting dark when we left our new resting place by the side of the road, having arrived there after not travelling very far during the previous day. We left in a hurry. The wagon in front of ours carried a live calf the drivers had 'organized' somewhere during the day. It was kicking and struggling to get free until in the end the driver, worried that it would escape, jumped off the cart and killed the poor creature by cutting its throat. As we neared the main road the calf's blood was still dripping from the wagon, colouring the dust ahead of us.

It was quite dark when we heard the sound of Russian aircraft which slowly circled us several times before dropping their flares,

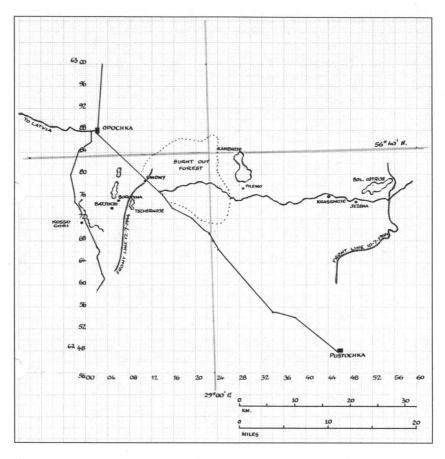

'Opochka'.

so that the countryside around us was as light as day. We expected their bombs to fall at any moment and listened nervously for them, but the aircraft passed directly overhead and continued on their way without troubling us which made us think that this time we had escaped their attention. But we were wrong.

We continued slowly along the packed road and soon afterwards heard a second wave of Russian aircraft approaching from the east. Once more we were lit up by their flares and waited for the fall of bombs – this time we did not wait in vain. The moment we heard the swishing sound in the air, we dropped down beside the wagons and the bombs exploded with ear-splitting reports around us. I felt a powerful blow on my right side which threw me under my wagon. My horse leaped forward and nearly pulled the wagon onto me, but I managed to grab it and was dragged along, thereby escaping being run over by the wheels. When the bombing came to an end and the horses stopped I tried to sit up, but my entire body ached and I remained lying by the roadside. My nose was bleeding and I had a large cut on my left forearm. I could not find any other wounds, but my ears were ringing and I felt dizzy.[10]

My friend Lazdans had fared worse.[11] Bomb fragments had hit him in the buttocks; his trousers had been ripped apart and were filled with blood. He lay at the roadside moaning and cursing in pain until a dog-drawn cart arrived and Lazdans was taken away. A German drove me back to the border of Latvia in a car, offering me a drink from a bottle of wine while cursing the Russians who gave us no peace, even at night. We passed through the village of Krasnoje which had suffered in the same Russian air attack. There were overturned wagons and dead horses at the roadside, the village was burning and clouds of sparks flew over the road which was still packed with traffic.

The German took me across the border into Latvia and to the hospital at Baranova where I was allowed to rest for the night. The next day, after an examination by a doctor who found that I had no internal injuries, I returned to the Supply Unit and began the long trek through Latgale and Vidzeme.

Notes

1 I heard later that they had been Russians.

2 Legionnaires slang for our quick-firing MG.

3 I later met one of the survivors of this massacre in the POW camp at Zedelghem in Belgium. He had been wounded in both arms and had remained down in the hollow smearing his head with blood. The Russians eventually stopped firing, came down from the hill and bayoneted all the wounded. Although he was kicked he had remained motionless and thus escaped with his life. He had managed to crawl away and reach some Latvian unit.

4 Translator.

5 This was the commander of the 15th Latvian SS Division Heilmann. On the same day he had shot several Latvian Legionnaires who had strayed from their units or had deserted them.

6 It is possible that the burnt-out forest ended sooner, but I know that we passed through it that night.

7 It is possible that the new front line positions which we occupied that morning were near a railway line. I seem to remember crossing some rails shortly before entering the trenches.

8 The Divisional Headquarters might have only been our Regimental Headquarters, but I am sure that some sort of command headquarters of the Latvian Legion was in the village.

9 My friend the Corporal was called either Andersons or Andermanis, and I seem to remember that he came from Sigulda. I have not been able to ascertain his fate and I am convinced that he died of his wounds later.

10 The Supply Unit of our company suffered most in this attack. The bombs killed our cook who had remained sitting on his field kitchen during the attack, and a couple of other men. Several of the wagons were destroyed and the horses were dead. Afterwards, during the withdrawal through Latvia, the unit was down to only two or three wagons.

11 Peteris Lazdans from the parish of Kalups in the district of Daugavapils. I met him after the war at the prisoner-of-war camp at Zedelghem in Belgium. He was still limping as a result of his injury.

Chapter 15

With Battle Group Jeckeln – Fighting in Estonia and Latvia, August to September 1944

When I rejoined the Supply Unit of our company there were only two wagons left from the previous ten or twelve. The men were resting in some bushes after the long drive through the previous night, and awaiting further orders.

The evening was warm as we moved off southwards, the carts overloaded with all that remained from our unit's supplies and which were considered the most useful. The drivers did not sit on the wagons but walked alongside them, with an extra horse tied behind one of them. It had suffered minor injuries during the air raid and it was hoped that it would recover. On reaching Stiglova we had to wait for a while near a church for our turn to continue. While there we saw a small light in the sky, like a star, approaching us from the south. The light progressed steadily but its path was slightly erratic and it made no sound in the quiet of that night. It could not have been an aircraft as they did not have navigation lights in wartime, so whatever it was remains a mystery.

Early in the morning we crossed the Rezekne highway at Berzgale and continued on our way through Ragauka, Driceni and then headed north. Expecting to go round the northern end of Lake Lubanas, we went through Bikava but from there once more turned south. On reaching the southern end of the lake we turned west to Varaklani. We had been driving for a couple of days by then, with only a few short rests by the roadside. The injured horse did not seem to have improved, although it still limped along behind one of the carts. The constant movement was not doing the animal any good and what it really needed was a decent rest to heal its wounds. We sold the horse to a farmer near Varaklani for a couple of bottles of vodka.

Most of our route was along small country roads. The larger highways were already crowded by the carts of Latgallian farmers who were leaving their homes and fleeing from the advancing Red Army. Those who remained behind were either Communist sympathizers or were too old to leave their homes. The long columns of refugees on the main roads were often attacked by Russian aircraft, which killed and injured a lot of people and horses with machine-gun fire and bombs. On the smaller roads we were comparatively safe. All the time we could hear the rumble of guns coming from the east where the Germans were fighting a desperate battle against the Red Army which was trying to advance further into Latvia.

From Varaklani we drove along the road to Madona, but before we reached the town we turned north heading for Lubana, where we stopped for a whole day in a wood, resting and awaiting further orders. We slept outside under the wagons and as we had plenty of food and drink from the Company's supplies, we were quite content with the war. Lake Lubana and its surrounding swamps protected us from any enemy approaching from the east. We had also left the River Aiviekate behind us and this formed another natural barrier against advancing Russians.

Continuing our journey we passed through a large forest and skirted the northern edge of an impassable swamp before emerging in the more open region of Vidzeme in central Latvia. It seemed that the Russian advance was expected to pass through the forest as many of the trees on both sides of the road had sticks of explosive tied to their trunks in readiness for felling them to slow the enemy. The partisans had been active even here. We saw a couple of graves by the roadside, each with a simple cross and a German helmet.

We spent the next few days driving through Vidzeme. No one really seemed to know our destination until, at the end of July, a new order arrived. Only one man per cart was to be left with the Supply Unit, while the rest of us were to assemble at the roadside. There we were formed into platoons and began the march south. We made good progress, passed through Laubere and one afternoon arrived in Koknese. After a short wait we were lined up and some fifty names were called out of those who were to be separated from the rest. All the Legionnaires selected from the ranks of our regiment were lined up on the road and told to wait for our German Army transport. While we were waiting I wandered into an orchard and found some blackcurrant bushes which were full of luscious fruit. The berries were very sweet and ripe, and I made a real feast of them.

When the trucks arrived we boarded them and set off straight away. The drive lasted some three hours, by which time we had reached Divisional Headquarters, about 20 miles from Riga, where we were to spend the night.

At the evening roll-call the officer read out the names of those who were to be decorated with the Iron Cross the next morning, and my name was among them. I had known nothing about this and the award came as a complete surprise. One of our officers had recommended me for my attempt to destroy the Russian machine gun on 10 July when most of our company were falling back from the surprise ambush. I had failed in my attempt, but at least I had tried.

We spent the night in a barn, sleeping in the hay, and were woken quite early. After breakfast and a general tidying up, everyone at Divisional Headquarters lined up in the open forest clearing. The Divisional Commander inspected the parade and then ordered those being awarded the Iron Cross to step forward from the ranks. About twenty men did so. The Divisional Commander personally attached the Crosses to our buttonholes, shook us each by the hand and expressed his congratulations.

We did not remain at the Headquarters much longer, were soon boarding the trucks and were on our way to Riga. People at the roadside waved and cheered and when we arrived in the town we were received like heroes – the people were under the impression we were coming directly from the front line. They also thought that we were there to defend the capital against the Russians, who had taken Jelgava in a surprise tank attack a couple of days earlier. The enemy had even managed to reach the sea west of Riga, thus cutting Latvia in half. Naturally the people were anxious and received us with open hearts. They threw packets of cigarettes into the trucks and girls decorated the Legionnaires with flowers. It was the custom in the German Army to wear the Iron Cross tied to the buttonhole for the first twenty-four hours and so the newly decorated men, I among them, received the most attention.

Our triumphal drive ended at the de-lousing unit where we had a shower and our uniforms were passed through decontamination ovens. Feeling clean and fresh we ended the day at the artillery barracks where we were to be stationed. The new unit was called 'Battlegroup Jeckeln'[1] and was composed of the best men from both of the Latvian divisions. We were to remain in Riga under the direct command of General Jeckeln and would be assigned special duties.

The next day we were completely re-equipped. We received new Panzer Grenadier uniforms, and the best quality arms and equipment. We had our meals with a German unit nearby and could go out of the barracks almost every evening. On the other hand the discipline and training for the first few days was very strict. We were trained in boarding and dismounting from our trucks as quickly as possible, before spreading out on both sides of the road in battle formation. We familiarized ourselves with the new weapons. The light machine guns were magazine-fed British Bren guns, made in Czechoslovakia; we also had Czech machine pistols and grenade attachments for our rifles. The officers of our company were battle-experienced veterans who had served and survived on the Eastern Front since the early days of the war. Nearly every day we drove out into the countryside near Riga to train. After about a week the discipline was relaxed a little, we were allowed more freedom and when out of sight of the officers sat about in the woods waiting to be driven home again. When the General Inspector of the Latvian Legion visited us he told us that our direct task would be the defence of the capital, but we knew that we would be used wherever necessary and did not really believe him.

On the morning of 11 August 1944 we left the artillery barracks for training as usual but were recalled at about 10 o'clock and told to prepare to leave at once in battle order. After a hurried meal and ammunition issue we boarded our trucks and left Riga around midday heading north. The drive lasted all afternoon. When we finally stopped we were near the Estonian border. After resting until nightfall in a wood, General Jeckeln himself came to see us.

He arrived in a light Fiesler Storch aircraft from Riga and after inspecting the assembled unit told us about our task. The Russians had broken through on the front line somewhere north of Latvia and their tank wedge was at present trying to cross Estonia from Verro to the sea. Our job would be to delay the enemy's progress until the arrival of larger German forces which were being moved to stop the Russian advance. A little later the other units comprising Battlegroup Jeckeln arrived from Riga. These consisted of a German military police company and a company of anti-tank guns. While waiting we received our daily food ration and a special issue of combat rations for the next day.

Once it was dark we once again boarded our trucks and drove off towards the north. We drove slowly all night and were further delayed by an air attack. The aircraft missed us but bombed the road about a mile ahead. Prepared for any eventuality, we dismounted and took cover in some bushes to await the departure of the enemy planes. Continuing on our way we passed some burning houses and supply trucks which had been hit by enemy bombs, and congratulated ourselves on our lucky escape.

The early morning of 12 August 1944 was clear and sunny as we drove through the highlands of Estonia admiring the beautiful view, all the time keeping our eyes open for Russian aircraft. An hour later thick fog descended over the countryside slowing us down, but around breakfast time we reached our destination, dismounted and left the lorries on the road.

Everything was quiet and nothing indicated the presence of Russians where, according to our orders, we were to take up defensive positions. The officer commanding our platoon knew some Estonian and obtained useful information about the countryside from the local inhabitants. The Estonians seemed to know that the Red Army was approaching. They were loading some carts with their belongings and the women were crying. It was clear they did not intend to stay there under Communist rule so were preparing to leave their farms and become refugees.

We did not know exactly where the enemy were and could not see very far in the fog. The officers indicated the general line we were to defend and after that it was the job of the platoon commanders to position their men in the best possible way. I split my platoon into three sections and placed each of these in the cover of some bushes about 400 yards apart. All that remained now was to watch for signs of the enemy. In the morning we had found out that the rifle grenades did not quite fit their rifle attachments. I used the time while waiting to scrape some of the plastic off so that they would fit. We did not intend to get too involved with the Russians – after a surprise ambush we were to withdraw and form a new line of defence when the enemy recovered and sent his tanks forward.

The waiting continued until midday and then we received the order to pull out. The Russian tank column had changed its course and we were to be moved to another position to intercept it. Half an hour's drive brought us there and this time we could hear the noise of battle nearby when we dismounted from our trucks, spread out in a field and started to advance towards a low range of hills.

The German military police company were on the left, we Latvians were in the centre and the anti-tank guns were on the right. The guns were towed straight to the top of the hills and opened fire right away. When we reached the hilltop and could see the country on the other side we realized why the guns were so quick off the mark. They had plenty to shoot at. The undulating country was full of Red Army tanks and trucks. It appeared that our arrival had come as a complete surprise to the Russians. The tanks and trucks were immobilized from the air by a score of Stuka dive-bombers, diving and firing their anti-tank cannons, dropping bombs and machine-gunning the tank crews and Russian infantry.[2] Now our anti-tank and machine guns added to the enemy's discomfort.

As long as the aircraft were attacking the enemy could not move, but when the Stukas departed to refuel the Russians started to fire on us. They soon found out the positions of our anti-tank guns and knocked them out one after another. Until then we had been spectators, but now it was our turn to draw the enemy's attention. They concentrated the firepower of all their tanks on the hills where we were. We had not had time to dig in and had to make the best of the cover available. The fire from the tanks was particularly unpleasant, the shells arriving without any warning and exploding among us with ear-splitting noise. We lost several men as a result of this fire, but when the tanks tried to approach us they were met by anti-tank rocket projectiles fired by the German military police company and withdrew leaving two tanks smoking a hundred yards in front of us. The crews were shot down when they attempted to leave the burning tanks. Several more tanks were already burning in the background, victims of the Stukas, sending up great columns of smoke in the still air. After this the Russian tanks kept back while their infantry tried to rush our positions, but they were mown down by our well-concealed machine guns. The Red soldiers who were still alive ran back despite the shouts of their political commissars who, in the end, fired on their own men from the rear with machine pistols. Then the Russians seemed to change their minds. They probably realized that they were dealing with an small unit, and apparently decided that the best course to take was to leave us alone. The enemy withdrew and started to move in a different direction, bypassing our positions on the left.

I had been hit by a small piece of metal while the tanks were firing at us. The shell fragment went right through my left cheek, broke off half a tooth and lacerated my tongue. In the excitement of battle I had not been aware of it but now the whole side of my head throbbed with pain and my cheek was so swollen that my left eye was nearly closed. The company's medical orderly had a look at my wound, dressed it and completed a wounded label which he tied to my tunic before sending me to the rear. The rest of the battle group were also preparing to retreat. Our transport had already driven up but I had to walk back to the casualty collecting station. Crossing the fields I could clearly see the Russian bullets flying through the cornfields and knocking down the stalks in straight lines. Further on the enemy bombarded our men with salvoes from their mobile rocket launchers which they had brought up with them.

After about a mile's walk I reached the casualty collecting station in an Estonian village, where I had to wait for transport. During this time the Russians got quite close. Their tanks had approached through the woods and started to fire into the village. All of a sudden the roadside ditches were full of German officers taking cover. It might have been amusing to watch but very soon I found myself in danger from shrapnel and machine-gun fire and had to take cover as well. Fortunately the tanks did not come any closer to the village and soon departed leaving a couple of burning houses. A unit of Russian SS men passed through the village moving up to the front to reinforce the thin line of defence. These men were all volunteers and were therefore expected to be trustworthy. If they were captured by the Russians they would be shot as traitors, and yet, for no apparent reason, we regarded them with suspicion. This suspicion was fully justified – I heard later that the Russian SS men had shot their officers and deserted to the enemy.

Transport for the wounded arrived in the evening and I was soon on my way back to Latvia. During the journey we passed a large number of German tanks and infantry of the 'Viking' SS Division, and other army units. These were the German reserves moving up to stop the Red Army's advance into Estonia.

I was eventually dropped off at Smiltene where I spent a couple of days convalescing at the overflowing military hospital. Then, one morning, after an influx of more wounded, I was given marching orders back to my unit. No one knew where Battlegroup Jeckeln was and therefore my orders were made out to report to the Riga artillery barracks where the Company still had its headquarters staff.

First of all I boarded the narrow-gauge train from Smiltene to Valmiera and managed to get into an empty goods wagon for the journey to Riga. I made myself comfortable on some straw and went to sleep straight away. When I woke up the train was standing in the station at Cesis. On opening the doors I saw two young men walking along the platform, one of whom asked if they could join me. They told me that they had just been called up and were on their way to report at Riga. They had several bottles of drink and a whole ham with them, and we spent the night sitting comfortably around their suitcase with a candle on it eating, drinking and talking.

When the train reached Riga the following morning it did not stop at the main station but carried on slowly through the town and across the bridges, finally stopping at Tornakalns. This suited me well. I had already removed the large plaster from my cheek which had returned to its normal size. Without rousing suspicion I could get off the train and go to my mother at work for the keys to our flat.

I spent a couple of days at home resting and cleaning my uniform, rifle and equipment. I could not stay long as my posting order had already expired and I had to report to the artillery barracks whether I liked it or not.

The only people there were the Company Clerk and a couple of men. No one knew for sure where the Company was and for the present I was to remain at the barracks to take my turn guarding the unit's property and equipment. Most of the men had left their personal belongings there thinking they would soon be back.

I returned to the barracks on 17 August 1944 and remained in Riga for the next three weeks. I was able to visit my home whenever I liked. This was a rare opportunity as leave was officially cancelled for all troops in view of the serious situation in Latvia. The enemy had already occupied half the country and it was only the heroic stand of German and Latvian forces that was keeping them from overrunning it altogether. There were frequent Russian air raids on Riga which, thanks to our anti-aircraft guns, did not do much damage. Nearly every day Russian reconnaissance aircraft flew over the town, but were driven off by anti-aircraft fire from numerous guns. Riga was full of refugees from eastern and southern Latvia which the enemy already occupied. Many people were leaving the country and heading for Germany.

I spent the rest of the month in Riga waiting for news of the Company. In early September the Sergeant Major arrived from the front to collect any men who were still in Riga. He told us what the Company had done since the action in Estonia. After leaving Verro they had been in the front line near Ape in Latvia where they had seen some heavy fighting but had been able to hold their own against persistent Russian attacks. For the last week the Company had been with the 19th Latvian SS Division manning the front line in central Latvia. The Sergeant Major only had a day in town before taking us all back to the Company to report for duty.

While our posting orders were being prepared I managed to get leave for a couple of hours and went to our flat to say goodbye to my mother. Unfortunately she was not at home and I did not have time to wait for her return. After writing a short explanatory note and eating some bread and jam, I left home for the last time, although I did not know it then and expected to return in the near future.

We boarded a train that same evening and set off on our journey. After a couple of hours we arrived at Ieriki where we were to change trains. We slept in the waiting room until late morning only to discover that our train had left without us, but we did not mind waiting for the next one. We sat around playing cards for most of the day and even managed to get two women to join us. Early that evening we started on a serious drinking session as someone still had some coupons with him and we used these to obtain drink. Later a local farmer joined us bringing with him a whole suitcase full of bottles. By this time we had completely forgotten about our orders and were in no condition to board the train when it arrived and left without us. The drinking and singing went on until late into the night and we finally slept once more in the waiting room.

When morning came the Stationmaster had had enough of us and called the local Military Police. They stopped the next train passing through the station and sent us on our way. The entire train consisted of flatbed trucks so we had to sit out in the cold wind for the whole journey. Another group of soldiers was travelling on another flatbed on the same train. They sat around a milk churn of home-distilled vodka, drinking and singing. To keep warm one of them started to run from one end of the train to the other, jumping over the coupling spaces. But he did not manage to get far before falling between two of the flatbeds and was promptly run over. The train stopped, his mutilated body was recovered and wrapped in a ground sheet, and we were once more on our way.

When we got off the train a couple of hours later the Sergeant Major realized that he had left his briefcase at Ieriki. He did not dare to return to the Company without all the documents and we agreed a plan of action. I, as the only one who could speak German, was to go back to Ieriki and collect the briefcase. The rest of them were to wait for me on a farm a couple of miles from the station before carrying on to the front line together.

The Sergeant Major wrote out my orders and I boarded a return train which was better than the last one. I slept on straw all the way back in a wagon full of horses, recovered the briefcase and in the evening of the next day returned to the waiting group. We spent one more night of freedom sleeping in a barn and only then completed the journey to the front line. It had taken us about five days to travel about a hundred miles, which was quite an achievement.

For the time being I was assigned to a reserve section, which was accommodated in the cellar of a farmhouse about half a mile behind the front-line trenches. They stretched along a line of low hills giving our men the best possible view of enemy movements. The Russians in this sector were comparatively quiet, limiting their activities to ineffective small-arms and mortar fire, and patrolling in no-man's-land at night. As usual Russian aircraft were busy at night, bombing our supply routes while trying to avoid our anti-aircraft fire.

One day we captured a Russian pilot who had been shot down the previous night and tried to cross the front line in daylight. He was a young man and shook with fear when our lads escorted him to the rear. Seeing the SS insignia he expected to be shot straight away and could hardly believe that we would let him live. After a cigarette and a drink, however, he became quite talkative and cursed the way the Red Army treated its men.

The following night our group was ordered to go out into no-man's-land in front of our trenches to observe the enemy. We set off late that evening, crossed our trenches and then moved very quietly and slowly towards the ruins of a farmhouse. As there was a possibility that the Russians might be there before us we stopped and listened for a whole hour lying on the frosty ground. But we could not detect any sound in the quiet of the night to indicate the presence of the enemy. Eventually our leader decided to move in. We stood up, shook our frozen legs and, with our weapons at the ready, we quietly entered the ruins. The house had been burned down and the floor had collapsed into the cellar. Two men were stationed outside while the rest of us sat in the cellar trying to keep warm and waiting for morning to come.

The night passed without any incidents and as the sun rose the two sentries were withdrawn into the cellar as they were too exposed and we could, in any case, see everything we needed through the small windows of the cellar.

Around breakfast time our artillery started firing ranging rounds along the Russian front line. The shells crept nearer and nearer to us until we expected the next salvo to fall right on top of the farm. It would have been impossible to move out of the cellar and seek better cover, and we had to rely on our good luck. When the shells arrived and exploded on the ruins we were showered with bricks and rubble but did not suffer any casualties. We didn't like being fired on by our own guns, but on the other hand we reasoned that it would convince the Russians the farm was not occupied, and we should be left in peace all day by the enemy.

Later that day we heard the Russians sawing wood in the forest directly in front of us, and also some hammering and shouting. They were obviously unaware of our presence and were getting on with building bunkers and fortifications. Through binoculars we could see a Russian soldier digging a slit trench right in the middle of a field. When he had finished he carefully camouflaged it and slowly strolled back to the woods. It would have been easy to have shot him but we did not dare give away our presence. Instead, we carefully noted the position of the trench so that our patrols could deal with the Russian listening post the following night.

Once it was dark we left the ruins and dug a well-concealed position for our machine gun in the orchard. Around midnight our replacements arrived and, after pointing out the direction of the enemy to them, we left the ruined farm. When we reached our own lines we reported to the Company Commander and went down into the cellar once more to sleep.

We spent the next day resting. Someone managed to 'organize' a little flour and a few eggs, and we made a real feast of pancakes with some jam which we had found in the farm's larder. We slept all afternoon but in the evening were ordered to join the neighbouring company in the trenches.

Once more the front line was being withdrawn a couple of miles and two groups of Legionnaires were to remain in the trenches as a rearguard. When we arrived the Company had already left. A sergeant showed us the part of the line that we were to man and left wishing us the best of luck.

It was a dark and windy autumn night. The unfamiliar surroundings and the knowledge that we were on our own in trenches normally occupied by a whole company made us nervous and suspicious of any noise. We would have liked to have sent up some flares to see what lay ahead, but did not dare in case it aroused the enemy. All we could do was walk along our sector of trenches firing off the occasional shot to maintain the impression of a fully manned front line. Once more I had a machine gun and spent the long night lugging it from place to place, firing into the darkness, reloading the magazine and watching for any signs of Russian patrols approaching our trenches.

By first light I was frozen and shivering, and my eyes kept closing. Then I heard from no-man's-land a sound which had me instantly alert. There, somewhere in the bushes to our front, I could clearly distinguish a Russian voice calling out instructions in an agitated manner. The next moment a salvo of shells landed somewhere behind us and the Russian started shouting again. Another salvo of shells exploded moments later and now it became clear that the Russian was correcting the enemy's artillery. It also seemed likely that the Russians were preparing to attack, but because of the bushes to our immediate front, we could not actually see the approach of the enemy. I could still hear the Russian's voice and tried unsuccessfully to silence him by firing into the bushes. Very soon shells were exploding right on top of us, with anti-tank guns and mortars joining in. With the bombardment really heavy now all we could do was cower in the trenches waiting for it to end and the infantry assault to begin. After bringing up extra ammunition and preparing hand grenades we were ready.

The concentrated shell and mortar fire lasted about fifteen minutes before ending abruptly. At the same moment we could see enemy infantry emerging from the bushes and running towards us. Everything now depended on us – the moment of truth had arrived. Luckily the Russian artillery and mortar fire had lifted to our rear so they did not hit their own men, and to prevent our reserves from reaching the threatened front line. We were still under fire from Russian machine guns but had to ignore them. When we saw the enemy they were about 300 yards away and at that moment we started firing. The first burst from my machine gun fell short – I could see the grass and earth spurting up in front of the Russians. A quick adjustment of my aim brought results and with my next burst several Ivans fell as if hit by an invisible hand; three of them remained motionless on the ground, while a fourth one tried to crawl into the cover of some bushes but did not get far before collapsing.

Although suffering heavy losses the Russians kept coming forward, but when the scattered groups of enemy soldiers were only about 80 yards from us they came upon an invisible obstacle which stopped them in their tracks. There, in front of our trenches, sappers had cut down some young trees, leaving the short stumps hidden in the grass, and had attached lengths of barbed wire to them. As the Russians advanced across the belt of barbed wire, we were able to pick them off with ease. By now they were also within range of our hand grenades and very soon those Ivans who were still alive started to run back in panic. Very few of them reached the cover of the bushes and many dead and wounded littered the ground in front of our trenches.

We were excited and jubilant, shouting to each other and continuing to fire into the bushes. Any enemy wounded who were still moving in no-man's-land were shot dead. The Company Commander walked along the trench distributing cigarettes and congratulating the men. We hoped that the Russians would not attack a second time but they thought differently.

Half an hour later we once again heard their forward observation officer directing the enemy's batteries and down came the shells a short while later. For the first quarter of an hour their fire was directed at the barbed wire, after which the shells fell once more on the front line. We crouched in the trench waiting for the end of the bombardment and the next attack. While cowering from the shellfire I had my right hand above my head holding on to the top of one of the trench support posts. A small splinter hit it and passed through my palm and although I did not feel any pain, the impact was like a heavy blow and then my hand became numb. I could not hold the machine gun any longer and handed it over to my No. 2, taking his place myself. I managed to stop the flow of blood somewhat by bandaging it and that was all I could do for the time being.

When the next enemy attack came my job was to hand full magazines to the new No. 1 on the gun. The Russians must have expected to get through the barbed wire without much difficulty, but they did not even get to it. During the preliminary bombardment one of our machine guns had taken up a new position – right in the middle of no-man's-land and well in front of our trenches. Even as the enemy troops started advancing in the open this gun began firing long bursts. The surprise was complete and the effect devastating. After losing many men to our concentrated fire, the Red soldiers turned and ran back. This time we knew that we had won the day.

During the action my hand had not bothered me much, but now it had become stiff and swollen, and the blood was soaking through the bandage. The Company Commander dressed it once more and sent me to the rear. I was to look after the Company's Supply Unit and stay with it until the situation concerning the new front line became clear.

I needed no encouragement to leave the front line. Being unable to defend myself I was scared and wanted to go as soon as possible. One of my friends had already been out in no-man's-land and had collected a Russian machine pistol from one of the dead. Before I left he handed me the weapon and I immediately felt better. I put the pistol's lanyard around my neck, grabbed the handle in my left fist and jumped out of the trench.

First I had to cross an open field and even as I was doing so the Russians renewed their bombardment. The shells exploded all around me so that for a moment I became confused and threw myself into a shell hole to seek shelter, but soon realized that I stood a good chance of being hit once more if I stayed there. I jumped out of the hole and ran quickly towards the trees. Once into the wood I was comparatively safe so rested for a while before going on. Beyond the wood, and after crossing some more fields, I reached a road where a car soon overtook me. It stopped and a Latvian officer offered me a lift. I was driven back 5 miles and I started to look for the Supply Unit, eventually being told that it had left that morning.

It took me the rest of the day to find Divisional Headquarters and even there nobody seemed to know the location of our Supply Unit, probably as all withdrawing units were still on the move. I therefore spent the night at Divisional Headquarters and in the morning I still could not find out where I was supposed to go. My hand was aching by now and I needed medical attention, which I decided to look for on my own. The nearest casualty collecting station was 10 miles away and I walked all the way. Fortunately it was a fine autumn day. While I was resting in some woods to the side of the road, a deserter passed quite close without seeing me. I could hear him approaching however quietly the man tried to move, and kept him in the sights of my machine pistol all the time. He must have been desperate and would not have hesitated to shoot me, thinking I would try to stop him.

I reached the casualty collecting station in the afternoon, had my bandage changed and was then sent to the railway station where a Red Cross train was already waiting. We reached Cesis after dark. Before being admitted to hospital, all the wounded were first sent for a shower and their clothes were de-loused.

I did not stay in Cesis for long. The very next day, with the Russians approaching, the hospital was evacuated. There was not enough transport for everyone so walking wounded had to walk along the highway towards Riga. When I left the hospital the enemy were quite near the town and I could hear the sounds of battle quite clearly. Some soldiers were looting a shop and passing out bottles of drink, tinned food and biscuits through a broken window. German sappers were busy blowing up the larger buildings and mining the streets.

The road to Riga was packed with troops, transport vehicles and wagons, and civilian refugees. It was actually quicker to walk through the fields off the road. Now and then Russian aircraft flew low along the road shooting up and bombing the traffic. There was no sign of the Luftwaffe so the enemy had a free hand.

After walking 5 miles or so the wounded were stopped and gathered together near a village. A short while later buses arrived and we boarded them for the drive to Riga, which we reached that night. The town was very quiet and dark, most of those out on the streets being soldiers. The civilians were all in their homes, behind blacked-out windows. Our bus stopped near the station and while the driver went to make enquiries about our destination I went into a house to ask for a drink as I was thirsty. I got the drink of water all right, but the attitude of the working-class family was quite different to the usual enthusiastic welcome reserved for Latvian Legionnaires. They expected the Russians to enter the town very soon and did not wish to be branded as collaborators.

When we set off again we were driven out of the city and finally, late that night, were housed in an empty textile mill on the outskirts of Riga, near Jugla. The looms of the factory had been removed from the long spinning and weaving halls, and in their place were beds for the wounded, who were to be examined by army doctors who decided each man's destination.

The sorting of the wounded continued throughout the next day. Some men were issued with orders to travel to Germany to convalesce, while those with minor injuries were ordered to report to local hospitals, presumably for re-employment at the front line in the near future.

I did not want to stay in Latvia any longer. It was obvious to me by now that the Germans were unable to stop the Russian advance and I had no wish to be killed or taken prisoner by the enemy. I had also passed beyond the heroic stage which would have urged me to remain out of patriotism and sense of duty to fight to the end. All I wanted was to preserve my life and get away from the constant threat of capture by the Russians. When I was handed my travel warrant I was glad to have it and realized that my future depended on that one piece of paper.

*   *   *

In the early hours of the following morning we boarded the buses once more and after a drive through the still sleeping town, reached the harbour where we were shown the large ship which was waiting for us. Before boarding it we had to leave all our arms on the quayside. I was therefore forced to part with the machine pistol, but somehow managed to keep two egg-shaped hand grenades. I also found a dock worker and asked him to post a letter to my mother which I had written the previous night with my left hand, but had not been able to find a post box. In the letter I explained what had happened, urged my mother to emigrate to Germany and told her not to worry about my hand.

It was still dark when I climbed the gangplank and handed in my boarding pass. No one bothered to direct people to their quarters as the ship seemed to be full already. The holds were crammed to capacity with wounded soldiers and civilian refugees. Many soldiers were making themselves as comfortable as possible on deck and I joined them. After finding a good place under a tarpaulin protecting one of the hold covers I decided to stay there for the voyage. I was aware of the possibility of attack by Russian submarines and aircraft, and this seemed to me to be the safest place. I could see new transports still arriving at the quayside and the stream of soldiers boarding the ship seemed endless. The Germans were glad to leave Latvia and return to their 'Fatherland'. Whereas they laughed and joked, passed around bottles of drink and were merry, the Latvians on board were more restrained and serious. They all realized that they were leaving their country, if not for ever, then certainly for a considerable time to come.

The loading of the ship did not finish until first light the next morning, then the last ropes were cast off and a tug began pulling the ship away from the quay and down the river towards the sea. I wanted to take one last look at Riga and to obtain a better view climbed up a ladder to one of the anti-aircraft guns. I could not see much in the pale grey light. One of the men in the German gun crew offered me the use of their binoculars. The view was decidedly better with the optical aid and I slowly scanned the panorama of the dark city, picking out familiar landmarks. I could not see our flat, but saw the neighbouring Russian Orthodox church and had to be satisfied with that. I thanked the German for the use of the binoculars and he understandingly shook his head. 'Der letzte Blick von Heimat, nicht wahr?' – the last glimpse of home. I did not feel like talking at that moment. It was Monday, 25 September 1944, and I was leaving Riga and Latvia, a Latvia which had failed to keep out the Russian reign of terror already engulfing half the land, and which would soon have complete control of the entire country and its people.

Notes
1 The supreme SS General in Latvian and other eastern regions.
2 This was the famous Tank Destroyer Squadron of Major Rudel. Their Stukas were specially equipped with anti-tank guns and could knock out tanks from the air.

Part V

Retreat from the Russians

Chapter 16

Germany, Recuperation and Return to the Legion, October to December 1944

It was broad daylight by the time the ship approached the open sea. The silhouette of Riga was becoming smaller and more indistinct, sinking gradually into the morning mist. We could see Bolderaja which was enclosed by dark pine forests and yellow sand dunes. After passing the two moles and lighthouse, we entered the Bay of Riga where we joined other ships which were already anchored to form a convoy for the voyage to Germany. The sea was calm and we remained at anchor awaiting the escort vessels of the German Navy.

After watching the lighthouse disappear in the distance I went to sleep under the tarpaulin and remained there until next morning. When I got up I could see a dark and wooded shoreline to the east. Perhaps this was my last glimpse of Latvia, but it is possible that by this time we were further south and the coast was that of Lithuania or East Prussia. After standing in a queue for some time I received my portion of dinner. The sea was quite rough by now and the ship rocked about a good deal. I went for a walk along the deck towards the prow of the ship, but the movement there was even more pronounced and made me feel a little seasick. Returning to my place amidships I lay down and immediately felt better. I spent the rest of the day sleeping and thinking about the future, about home and the people I had left behind in Latvia.

When I next lifted my corner of the tarpaulin I could see a setting

141

moon spreading its light over the waves. It was a beautiful sight but I was not really in the mood to enjoy it. From the position of the moon and stars I could see that morning was not far away. I refused the invitation of my German companions to join them in a card game under the propped-up tarpaulin by the light of a candle, and awaited the sunrise sitting on the deck.

At about 8 o'clock the ship entered the harbour of Dantzig.[1] I studied the people carefully, expecting them to look different to the people of Latvia, but could not detect any foreign elements in their appearance or behaviour. They were simply workers going to work – just the same as elsewhere in the world.

The ship berthed at the quayside and the first to be unloaded were the stretcher cases. The walking wounded had to wait their turn before eventually disembarking and being taken to a train for our journey to hospital.

The train started around dinner time and we were on the move for a couple of days, during which the train hardly ever stopped. We travelled south, along the Polish Corridor where sometimes great forests enclosed the track on both sides for hours. In open spaces the countryside was flat and featureless, stretching monotonously to the grey horizon. Later, when passing through industrial Silesia, I saw many steaming factories, dirty coal mines and smoking slag heaps. The railway became hemmed in by high mountains and we often passed through dark tunnels, all the time nearing the border with Czechoslovakia. The closely knit network of railways in this industrial land slowed us down considerably. We finally halted at a small country station which seemed very quiet – only the railway staff moved about the station in the deserted village. As we waited in the yard for our transport to the hospital, the village seemed so peaceful that it was hard to believe that there was a war going on. The well-kept flower beds were full of blooming asters and other autumn flowers, and the trees in the neighbouring orchard were loaded with apples gleaming in the moonlight.

When the trucks eventually arrived we were driven through the sleeping, mountainous countryside for some 5 miles to a large sanatorium where we were met by nuns in black uniforms and flowing white headdresses. We were tired from the long journey, but before we were allowed to enter the hospital we had to have a shower in lukewarm water which I did not enjoy. Only then was I permitted to get into bed and go to sleep between clean white sheets. It was Saturday, 30 September 1944.

The hospital was situated on the former border between Germany and Czechoslovakia and in peacetime had been a sanatorium and spa as its name implied – Bad Johannisbrunn. The nearest town was Troppau. I spent the next six weeks there. After discovering that I was of Latvian nationality, I was asked whether I would like to be transferred to a room reserved for foreigners, and I agreed. There I met a couple of Latvians and some other foreign nationals – all members of the German armed forces. The hospital staff consisted of local nuns and German Red Cross personnel. The chief surgeon was a middle-aged German who had served in Latvia in the First World War with the German Army. He had been favourably impressed by the Latvian people then and now showed special consideration towards me. He often questioned me about the conditions in Latvia and expressed the hope that I would be able to go home one day without fear of retribution for my service in the German Army.

Having had my arm in a sling for a fortnight the bandages and splints were removed, and I was ordered to report for work in the hospital kitchens. My right hand was quite stiff and useless, and needed exercise to recover. One of the Red Cross sisters massaged it every day and the exercise consisted of peeling potatoes. I did not like the painful massage but did not mind working. Among the kitchen staff were three young French girls and a Frenchman – a prisoner of war. During my stay I became quite friendly with them and discovered that they did not mind working for the Germans. Nearly every evening we walked out together for a mile or so to the neighbouring village of Kreuzberg. There we spent our spare time sitting in one of the two inns, drinking the weak wartime beer and singing with the village folk.

The local people were a mixed bunch – there were Germans, Poles and Czechs, but they seemed to get on quite well together. Their houses, however, were separated into two groups. The Germans and Czechs occupied the end of the village with the two inns, the street was clean and the houses were bright. But it was a different matter at the Polish end of the village. Once, when I ventured there in search of some home-grown tobacco, I found that the street was covered in mud, the people were dirty and the houses dilapidated. A large Catholic cross stood at this end of the village indicating that the inhabitants were religious.

The wounded helped in various jobs connected with the running and upkeep of the hospital, such as carrying full milk churns up the steep approach road into the kitchen and returning with the empties. One day a party of us went to help with retiling the roof of the doctor's house. Most of the work was light and we did not mind doing it. A couple of times we saw large formations of American aircraft flying past on their way to bomb German cities; in the woods we found many leaflets urging the local people to refuse to serve the Germans and giving the latest news from the front line. These were the only signs of war that I saw during my stay at Bad Johannisbrunn.

On 18 November the Latvians organized a celebration of our country's independence and were allowed to use a large room all night. We had plenty to eat and drink and a group of Latvian girls came from a neighbouring refugee camp to help in the celebration, but the party passed quietly. We had long since heard that Riga had fallen to the Russians on 13 October so that now only Courland[2] remained free from the Red terror. Our spirits were therefore low and the party seemed more in the nature of a remembrance service than a celebration.

A week later I was told that I would be discharged from the hospital in a couple of days' time. I did not want to go and went to see the Chief Surgeon to ask for a month's leave, which was due to me on account of the period of time I had spent with the Legion without home leave. The doctor agreed that I had some leave due, but told me frankly that he had already kept me at the hospital longer than necessary and could not extend my stay any longer. He advised me to go to my unit and apply for leave there.

I was discharged from hospital on 27 November and ordered to report for duty at Neuhammer in Czechoslovakia. After a day's train journey I arrived in Neuhammer and started to look for the Latvian Legion, but all I could find was a unit of Estonian Legionnaires. The officer in charge directed me to go to East Prussia, right across Germany, to Butow, and gave me the necessary travel warrant. The journey through Germany was very slow, with the train making frequent stops which were necessary to allow military trains the right of way – in some places the track had suffered bomb damage in night air raids and we had to wait until it was repaired. The stations were dark, cold and dirty. The signs of war were plain to see everywhere.

It took me three days to get to Berlin where I spent a day wandering through the city, using the opportunity to see something of the German capital. The sight was pretty depressing but the people showed little significant concern for the ruined buildings and seemed cheerful enough under the circumstances. Perhaps they were used to the nightly air raids, the shortage of food and the lack of heating in their homes. The shop windows were empty or displayed some non-rationed goods which no one wanted. There were long queues outside grocery stores where the women waited patiently to receive the meagre rations of food. The underground and overhead railways were functioning, although in many places the stations and tracks had been bombed and repaired. I visited the Latvian Refugee Centre seeking information about my mother, but her name was not on their card index and I therefore had to assume that she had remained in Riga under Communist rule.

When I arrived at Butow and went into the guardroom I received an unexpectedly hearty welcome. The NCO of the guard was one of the German corporals who had instructed me in Riga. He still had a photograph of the Guards Company in which we had both served in Riga on the wall of his room. After a drink or two the German advised me to try to obtain a posting somewhere else. The living conditions in Butow were poor – the men of the 15th Division were quartered in plywood huts which were half buried in the ground to keep the cold out. The fields and roads around the camp were waterlogged and muddy, and the men themselves looked dirty and apathetic. I was glad when I was ordered to go to Berent and report to the holding unit of the Latvian Legion.

I did not have to travel far. A day later I was established in a wooden hut in a small town awaiting further orders. Here all the Legionnaires returning from hospital were held for a period until they were re-equipped and sent to their units. I met some of my old friends and heard about others who were either in Latvia with the 19th Division or had died in the last turbulent months of 1944.

As soon as possible I sent in a home leave request for which I qualified on account of the time I had served with the Legion. We were supposed to have relatives in Germany to claim leave and although I did not have any, this was the least worry. I obtained an envelope with a postmark from somewhere in Germany, deleted the pencil-written name of the recipient and substituted my own. Then I wrote a letter to myself, supposedly coming from my uncle in Memingen in southern Germany, appended the letter to my leave request and handed them in to the Commanding Officer.

My leave started on 11 December 1944 and I had to report back for duty on 1 January 1945, which gave me three weeks freedom which I could spend as I liked. My travel permit was made out to Memingen which meant I could travel right across Germany and back. I had food coupons for three weeks and plenty of money – just before leaving hospital I had received my wages for the entire period I had spent there.

First of all I spent a couple of days in Berlin and then continued the slow journey south. It took about a week to reach Memingen where I told the local military authorities that my relative had moved. I therefore requested that my travel warrant be altered to Bad Johannisbrunn in Czechoslovakia where I intended to spend Christmas at the hospital.

During my journey through Germany I passed through many famous towns, but the cold weather prevented me from seeing much of them. I had to leave the train a couple of times to go to an air-raid shelter when the alarm sounded heralding the approach of Allied bombers, but every time the aircraft passed by without attacking. I had to walk into Munich following an air raid which had destroyed the railway line and time bombs were still exploding in the city when I boarded my connecting train. I spent a few hours walking up and down the station platform at Mozart's town of Salzburg, trying to keep warm in the cold wind while I awaited the arrival of my next train. The waiting rooms were too full to get in. I was lucky in Vienna where I helped a Red Cross sister in the soldiers' welfare rooms to carry in a cauldron of hot soup. For my efforts I was rewarded with a basinful of meat which the sister fished out from the bottom and pushed towards me with a wink. Another thing I noticed in Vienna were the lists of brothels displayed in the station's waiting room. There were separate lists for officers and other ranks, which seemed strange to me at the time. At one station, while running across the platform to catch a train, I was stopped by an officer who shouted at me for not saluting him. On seeing the silver wounded shield and the Iron Cross on my chest, he soon quietened down and allowed me to go without further questions.

When I arrived in Czechoslovakia, my first stop was at the village of Kreutzberg where I booked a room at a small hotel, the Goldgrube. I planned to stay there over Christmas and visit my friends at the hospital in Bad Johannisbrunn. I was warmly received at the hospital – the chief surgeon told me I could stay there if I wished and even sleep in my old room. I thanked him for the offer, but told him that I had already booked a room in the village. All my old friends were still there. Ruze, the Latvian war correspondent, was still diligently learning English, although the original purpose of this was no longer relevant. He had started to improve his knowledge of English in October when there was a request for English-speaking volunteers to join the German Army for the planned Ardennes offensive – Hitler's last gamble – which by now was already lost, but Ruze still continued with his lessons with an eye to the future.

I was also welcomed by my French friends and the POW even managed to produce a bottle of cognac to mark the occasion. I spent Christmas at the hospital and took part in all the celebrations, even being given the hospital's Christmas rations of drink and sweets. On returning to my hotel I was asked to join the landlord's family in their feast, and spent the next few days recovering from the celebrations and preparing to leave. On the way back to Berent I stopped off for another day in Berlin and left the town on New Year's Eve.

Notes
1 Modern Gdansk. (*LB*)
2 The north-western part of Latvia. (*LB*)

Chapter 17

1945 Diary

Introduction

This diary describes the everyday happenings in the 5th Company of the 3rd Sapper Regiment, Latvian Legion from 1 January to 3 May 1945 when I was taken prisoner by the Americans. Also included are some of my diary notes written in POW camps, mainly concerning the food situation and the various rumours circulating at the time.

By now our main concern was food. The rations were insufficient and so we were always trying to obtain something extra to eat – such supplementary rations were necessary to give us strength to wield the picks and spades while digging trenches and anti-tank ditches. This concern with food accounts for the almost daily references to rations. Even taking into account the extra food that we managed to get our hands on, most of us managed only one meal a day. We had the same concern with food as prisoners of war, and the diary faithfully records the amount I received. We even cooked and ate grass in the camp of Neuengamme. There was little nutritional value in the resulting green stew, but our main concern was to fill our empty stomachs. There were even dog biscuits for sale on the black market of the camp, although they were full of worms and unfit even for animals.

It required a great effort by us on the long march to reach the American forces and escape from the rapidly advancing Russians. Quite often during the longer stretches I felt like lying down at the side of the road and giving up. My legs ached, my boots rubbed my blistered feet and my eyes kept closing with fatigue. It required all

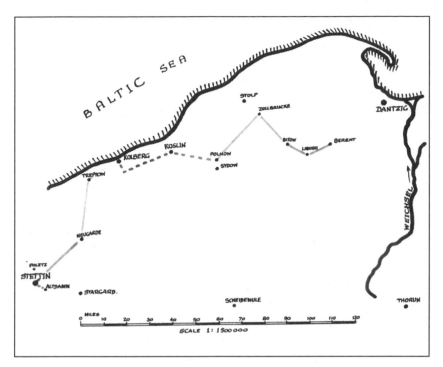

My movements through Pomerania,
December 1944 to February 1945.

my willpower to start again after every rest halt. I think that the
main driving force for us all was the fear of the Russians who were
not far behind us.

As regards the dissatisfaction and distrust of the Latvian officers
in the POW camps which I describe, I can only say that most
Legionnaires felt the same as I did. The suspicion that officers
obtained food illegally is supported by the case I describe. Attempts
to enforce discipline were considered as unnecessary interference in
the Legionnaires' private lives. On becoming prisoners of war we
considered ourselves free from the authority of officers, the
grounds for which were, perhaps, the loss of our homeland and the
hopelessness of our situation.

1 January 1945
Greeted the New Year at Berent. Arrived 31:12:1944 at 2300
hours. Spent all day waiting for orders posting me to my unit, but

without success. Exchanged tunics with Pommers and he added ½ a packet of tobacco. Wrote letters to Grants and Ruze. Thought of writing to Gaida but did not. Spirits high![1]

2 January 1945
Continued the waiting but nothing happened. Sold knitted underpants for RM60.00 and one packet of tobacco. Bought ten packets of cigarette papers @ RM0.50. Nothing special all day. Intended to manage on daily ration of food only. Chess.[2]

3 January 1945
Bought one loaf of bread for RM30.00 and ten cigarettes for RM30.00. Spent every free moment playing chess. Weather cold and damp. Continued to await orders.

4 January 1945
The day began as monotonous as all the previous ones, but I had a surprise in the evening – I received a New Year's greetings card from Gaida. Very pleased with this, although the card had only a few words on it. I am still waiting for my posting order, but not really bothered any more whether it comes today, tomorrow or after a longer time.

5 January 1945
Wrote a letter to Gaida this morning. The day passed as monotonously as all the others. Visited Rubauskis, who was ill in bed, in the afternoon. Did some reading and played chess in the evening.[3]

6 January 1945
Went to Battalion Headquarters concerning my posting order, but even they could not clarify the situation. However, I was told that I would be sent to Polnowa, and the papers would be sent to the Company in due course.

7 January 1945
At last, around 9 o'clock in the morning, my posting order arrived. Left Berent at 4:50 pm but only managed to get to Libush where we had to wait till 11:50 pm for a connecting train to Bitow. Visited the Soldiers' Club. The rooms were quite nicely appointed and we even managed to get a meal. Terrible lemonade!

8 January 1945

Slept until morning in Bitow and then continued the journey to Zollbrucke where we had to wait until 2:50 pm. Arrived at Polnowa at 4:30 pm, and got assigned to the 5th Company. Living in wooden huts. No light in the evening – electricity has not been laid on.[4]

9 January 1945

Peeled potatoes all day. Still, this is better than having to go out and dig anti-tank ditches in the cold, or freeze on exercises. Wrote to Gaida during the dinner hour and gave her my new address. The food situation here seems to be better than elsewhere. In the evening, from 5 pm, I was free but could not do anything on account of the lack of light.

10 January 1945

Did not do anything worthwhile in the morning. We were expecting a visit by the Divisional Commander, but he did not arrive. In the evening wrote a letter to Rubauskis. It is snowing and the weather is not to my liking. Went to sleep early – there was nothing else to do. An issue of clothing has begun.

11 January 1945

Took part in training in the morning. My hands were frozen stiff. Obtained some gloves later and in the evening was issued with a soldier's canteen. Took over as NCO on duty. Wrote to Ruze asking him to send 'Junda'.[5] In the evening the men in the Company received their monthly issue of toiletries, but I did not receive any as I arrived late.

12 January 1945

Duty NCO. At 11 am the Battalion Commander visited the Company and I had to report to him. Clear and starry night. Moderate frost.

13 January 1945

In the morning took part in special exercises for NCOs, but we did not do much. Rumours that the 15th Division would go to the front at the end of February, and that we would go with them.[6]

14 January 1945
Sunday. No work and no exercises. Instead we had to leave the barracks by 8:00 am to go to the dentist for a check-up of our teeth. Arrived at 9 am but had to wait a whole hour outside in the cold until the dentist came. Returned around 11 am and it was soon dinnertime. Wrote a letter to Lans in the afternoon.[7]

15 January 1945
Went to work in the morning. Not much enthusiasm for working, and we only moved sufficiently to keep warm. Back around 3 pm. I was told that in future I would not have to go out with the working parties, but could remain in camp as an instructor. Northern lights visible in the evening.

16 January 1945
Drill in the morning. The weather was quite cold and I felt sorry for the lads I was exercising. Nearly half of them have no gloves. My own hands and feet were freezing. In the evening a far-off rumbling could be heard – the bombardment of Dantzig. Played solo.

17 January 1945
Rumours started to go around today that the Russians had begun a major offensive along the entire Eastern Front. Snowstorm. Drill. Bread soup this evening which was so unappetizing that I cannot manage to eat my portion.

18 January 1945
An order came through that 80 per cent of the Company are to be employed in building defences, and I had to go out once more today. It is not cold, but the snowstorm is not to my liking. In the evening my feet were wet through. Read the newspaper to the whole platoon. Goulash for supper, but microscopic quantity.

19 January 1945
The Company Sergeant Major promised a Sunday off if we finish the allotted quota of work by tomorrow. Most of us do not believe him. After digging all day I felt quite tired in the evening. A clear day but getting cloudy towards the evening.[8]

20 January 1945

It seems that we will not get Sunday off after all as we started work in a new place. We have to march some 5 miles to get there. We are digging to increase the slope of a hill near a lake. Rumour has it that we have to finish the job in five days. Knocked off at 2 pm but tomorrow we will have to work until 4 pm.

21 January 1945

The Germans are noticeably worried by the Russian offensive and are trying to increase our work rate. We heard rumours that we have to finish this particular assignment by 24 January. The Russians are supposedly in Litzmanstadt; another rumour is that our men have left Thorun.

22 January 1945

Working on an anti-tank ditch. The work is urgent now and continues into the night. The Russians are supposed to be near Thorun. In the evening the Company Clerk took down the names of all those who could not march. Rumour has it that we may have to march to central Germany. We could hear the sounds of battle coming from the front line. Freezing.

23 January 1945

Foggy and cold. The work on the anti-tank ditch continues. Working from 8 am until 3 pm. Our lads in Thorun have been attacked by the Russians from the air. The food is getting worse every day on account of a shortage of potatoes. Received some soap this evening.

24 January 1945

I was about to leave for work when the Company Sergeant Major told me to stay behind and report to Battalion Headquarters. Arrived there about 10 am and received the Iron Cross certificate that I had requested from Berent. Late this evening, around 11 pm, the Sergeant announced that we should prepare to leave tomorrow.

25 January 1945

Received the official order to pack and prepared to leave. Dinner time came and then the evening, but we are still here. The early rumours were that we would have to march about 120 miles, and later, that we would go by train. Our destination is supposed to be Schneidemule. There are a lot of rumours flying about, and it is possible that there is some truth to all this.

26 January 1945

Our kit remains packed, but the order to leave does not come. Training began again in the morning and continued into the afternoon. The sky has been cloudy and the weather windy and cold. The conditions are becoming worse day by day. We have not received any tobacco for a couple of weeks and there seems to be no hope for improvement in the future.

27 January 1945

Training continued all day and we have not heard any more news about leaving. The Russians are supposed to be in Schneidemule. Snowing and windy. I have a bit of a cold and my throat is sore. I would not like to become seriously ill in the present situation.

28 January 1945

We were told first thing to repair and wash our uniforms. Then, around 10 am, a new order arrived to prepare for work. After working until 1:00 pm we were back by 2:30 pm. The weather is cold and windy and I am freezing. This evening a platoon of men was selected from the Company to serve with the 15th Division in the front line. I stay here for the time being.

29 January 1945

The men selected for front line leave about 1 am. I go to work in the morning. There is a snowstorm but it is not cold and I enjoy working. The job of building the anti-tank obstacle is nearing completion. On the way home I visited a farm where I bought a loaf of bread for RM10.00. In the evening we receive the tobacco ration for eight days: three cigars. Too little.

30 January 1945

I remain in the barracks because in the afternoon I have to take over as duty NCO. Wash my underclothes and pullover. The weather is clear and sunny. At 10 pm Hitler spoke on the radio but did not say anything of importance. It is rumoured that the Russian advance has been stopped.

31 January 1945
The order to prepare to leave came at around 9 am. We had our meal and left Hildegardshohe at 1 pm. We reached Polnowa by 2:30, were given 24-hour rations packs and left at 3:30 for Koslin. There was a snowstorm at the beginning of the march, later it was freezing, and then it started to thaw. Around 4:00 am (the next morning) we arrived in Koslin. Many of us were complaining that they could not go any further.

1 February 1945
In Koslin we were shown sleeping quarters in the loft of an army barracks. It was very cold there. Slept till 10 am. We were told that we would have to continue that evening. In the evening we were told that we would be staying for the night, so we settled down for sleep. Then the order to prepare to leave came at 11:00.

2 February 1945
We began marching to Kolberg at 1 am. The weather was very windy. Some of the men had small sleds on which they dragged their belongings, but they very soon had to discard them. It began to snow but then a thaw set in and we became wet through in no time. We left the main road about 7 miles before Kolberg and marched along minor roads. After another 8 miles we were billeted in some farms where we were given supper. We had marched 40 miles in sixteen hours.

3 February 1945
The farmer's wife is very kind and we get plenty to eat. For breakfast we have sausage, bread, jam, dripping and hot milk. Dinner: meat, potatoes, gravy and sauerkraut with cranberry sauce. We collected RM70.00 after dinner for our landlady, but had some trouble persuading her to accept it. We had the opportunity to sleep comfortably, rest and recover. Rumour has it that we are to continue on our way tomorrow.

4 February 1945
We do not go anywhere yet. I am idle all day. Play solo. The food is still as good as on the first day; besides we are given 24-hour

ration packs for three days and some cigarettes. There has been some stealing going on in the village. The Russians are supposedly at Prutz and Stargard.

5 February 1945
The day passed like all the others here. We helped the landlady to peel some potatoes and I managed to wash my feet. Two German girls came to visit us in the evening and Zeltkalns⁹ went off to see them home. Rumours that the 15th Division has been routed in battle, and we will have to go to the front line to take their place.

6 February 1945
First thing this morning I was assigned to work in the forest. We left the farm at 8 am and had to march 3 miles into the forest, returning at 4 pm. We were ordered to leave for another village some 5 miles from here straight away. The landlady boiled some milk for us and we left around 5 pm. The landlady at the new place was as kind as the previous one and our supper was magnificent. We could hear the distant sounds of battle to the west.

7 February 1945
I have got a cold, my head is aching and my lips are covered with cold sores. We do not do anything, but at 3 pm the company is ordered to parade on the road. Reading of the divisional order that anyone caught stealing will be shot. Someone has sold a pair of boots and this is forbidden too. We are not told anything about moving on. The electricity goes off at 8 pm and we have to go to sleep.

8 February 1945
Everyone has to provide details of our length of service in the Legion, and the various units we have served in. Volunteers for the Parachute Unit are supposed to leave soon. Receive wages for the month of February. There is an air raid at Kolberg in the evening, and to the west we can see distant flashes of anti-aircraft guns. Around 7 pm we see vivid flashes of light in a south-westerly direction. It seems that these could be naval guns. The Russian attack towards Stettin is continuing.

9 February 1945

We all have lice and decide to get rid of them. We mix quicksilver with lard and rub our bodies with the paste. The lice began to leave our clothes straight away, but in the evening we feel ill. It is possible we have quicksilver poisoning. Life goes on as usual without anything much happening. The Commanding Officer spoke to us and warned us of the consequences of stealing and selling army equipment.

10 February 1945

We slept all day and only got up early in the evening when we were asked by our landlord to help with threshing some corn. The threshing machine is primitive and the grain comes out mixed with chaff. We are told in the evening that tomorrow we will have to go out to work on an anti-tank obstacle.

11 February 1945

In the morning we were ordered to pack and prepare to leave. Then 11 am we were ordered to get ready for work. Left the farm at noon and arrived at the place we were to work at 2 pm after marching about 5 miles. We didn't have to do much and left for home at 4 pm arriving at 6 pm. The weather is very changeable: clear in the morning, then misty and some rain, which stopped in the evening. We slept fully dressed covered by our greatcoats so that we could leave at short notice.

12 February 1945

We did not have to work and spent all day at the farm. My teeth are aching and the medical orderly says that the cause is lack of vitamins. We have nothing to take to remedy the shortage. There are rumours going round that we are going by train from Kolberg to Wittenberg, and are only waiting for the wagons. All the sick and those who have not been fully trained are being posted to the 4th Battalion.

13 February 1945

My toothache persists and now I have a headache as well. At 2 pm the Company is lined up on the road and the CO announces that we must be prepared to leave at any moment. He also lectures us on how we should behave during the journey. By evening there is still no order to leave, so it will come either during the night or in the morning.

14 February 1945
The order to prepare to move comes at 10 am and we leave at 11 am and reach Kolberg around 1 pm. There were no stoves in the goods wagons so we started to remove some from another train, but attracted the attention of the Military Police. In the end we were allowed to keep the stoves, but had little comfort from them because they smoked so badly. We had an air alert at Treptow in spite of the cloudy weather.

15 February 1945
We arrived at Neuegarde during the night and stayed there all day. Late that evening the journey restarted and we reached Stettin in the evening. I am still feeling ill because of the continuous aching of my teeth and gums. I also have a festering sore on my face – many of us are suffering in the same way. The sores and toothache are allegedly due to a lack of vitamins. Rumours that we would be joining the 'Viking' Division. Arrived at Stettin at 8 pm and spent the night in the wagons.

16 February 1945
Around 10 am we moved on to Altdamm, a suburb of Stettin, where we leave the train. While waiting for further orders we are billeted in the loft of some stables. We are supposed to work on the defences around Stettin. We have to spend tonight here, but tomorrow we are to go into barracks. Clear and starry night. I am a little cold here sleeping on the bare boards.

17 February 1945
We stayed in the loft until midday and had potatoes and gravy for dinner. We left the town at 1 pm for our new quarters and had to walk some 2 miles before reaching a hutted camp. Evening came while we were making ourselves as comfortable as possible. We had electricity and our own kitchen, and were given some coffee. The night was clear and cold.

18 February 1945
We got up around 6 am and marched several miles to where we were to dig front-line trenches. The soil was sandy, the work progressed well and we quite enjoyed it. Throughout the day we saw considerable enemy air activity. This evening, on the way back to camp, we saw unending columns of refugees moving in the direction of Berlin. Poor food.

19 February 1945
We dug the trenches from 7 am to 3 pm. Tomorrow we are supposed to start working to a quota: ninety men have to dig and reinforce 80 metres of trench 1.10 m by 1.6 m, and then we can finish. During the day we could hear loud rumbles from the front line. German heavy artillery fired some ranging shells around Stettin. We were told that tomorrow we wouldn't get any soup, but instead were given a 24-hour ration pack and some cigarettes.

20 February 1945
The weather was clear and sunny, and we finished the work set us by midday. During the day the Russians attacked Stettin several times from the air, but in the evening, around 7 pm, the real attack began. It was a bright night, with flares floating down from enemy aircraft making it nearly as bright as day. The second wave of aircraft arrived 10 pm, and we could still hear the engine noise of the Russian aircraft for some time after this. Several bombs landed about half a mile from our camp.

21 February 1945
We began work to the accorded quota. Each man had to dig and reinforce about a yard and a half of trench. We finished work around 2:30 pm and were home by 4 pm. The morning was cloudy, but the sky had cleared by the evening. Around 9 pm a general alarm was sounded. We went out into the meadows surrounding the huts and sat down near a haystack and remained there for about half an hour. Then the 'All Clear' was sounded. One of the enemy planes was caught in the searchlight beam and unloaded its bombs in the field right on top of the haystack which we had left a short while earlier. Lucky escape.

22 February 1945

Finished work at 1 pm and the Company was paraded at 3 pm. The Company Commander announced the formation of a battle group led by Colonel Rusmanis, for which our company have to contribute thirty-five men. Ten men volunteered for the new unit and the rest will be appointed by the CO from the Company's list. In the evening, although the sky was cloudy, there was an air alert, but we were given the all clear half an hour later.

23 February 1945

The names for the battle group have not been announced, and we have heard nothing more about it. We finished work around midday, but even our dinner break was not free! On orders from the Company Commander we had drill for an hour. This evening, we had to do some singing and were supposed to parade for an evening roll-call, but this was postponed because of the rain. The men were bitter and upset, complaining that if they have to do drill in their free time there is no point working hard to finish work early.

24 February 1945

Nothing special happened. According to rumours Turkey has declared war on Germany and the British have started a major attack. The bread ration is 20 oz per day but we are not particularly hungry. The explanation for this may be that we are still living on the accumulated reserves of energy from the villages around Kolberg. I have some spots on my face and do not know the reason for them. The days are foggy but the nights are clear.

25 February 1945

Although it is Sunday we worked until midday. On getting back to camp there are rumours of a special issue of toilet requisites. The names of the men ordered for front-line duty are announced during the evening roll-call. They have to leave tomorrow at 9 am. Once more my name is not among them. Most of the men appointed to the battle group are old and have not seen any fighting. The weather is cloudy with rain about.

26 February 1945

It has rained all day and we arrive back wet through. I put my clothes out to dry but around 4 pm we all go to have a shower. Clean once more and clothes de-loused. Home 9 pm. Then we receive an extra issue of ½ pt of vodka, ½ pkt tobacco, two cigars and thirty cigarettes. I sold my vodka for RM40 and 4 oz smoked bacon. Many were drunk and made a great din until late in the night. Clearing clouds in the evening and the moon is shining.

27 February 1945

Some men were still drunk when we set off in the morning and had to stagger along as best they could. We finished work early. Received some soap this evening. The present Sergeant Major is being posted to another company and his place will be taken by Corporal Kalnins. With the help of some German drivers our kitchen staff have bought a cow. The cook is already promising a special soup tomorrow. He has plenty of meat now.

28 February 1945

I was duty NCO and remained in camp. A clear and spring-like day. One air attack at 4 pm and another at 8 pm. The Russian fighters fly low and shoot up the roads which are full of military and civilian traffic. In the evening one of the men allotted to the battle group returned and told us that Siderovs has been wounded in an air raid.

1 March 1945

We were shown a new work site in the orchard of a farm. As soon as we had begun to dig the trench a German captain arrived and ordered us to fill it in again. It seems that the local farmer bribed the officer to save his orchard from being dug up. We were sent elsewhere. According to rumour we are to leave on 4 March to either Dresden or Leipzig.

2 March 1945

A very strong wind blew all night and all day; in the morning there was even some snow on the ground. We have been working at the same place. Someone has found out where we can obtain potatoes, and we boil and eat them every day. The soup has been better lately. We have 'organized' a couple of cows from the cattle being driven past with the permission of the men in charge of them as they had no idea how many cows they had in the first place.

3 March 1945

The weather was clear and spring-like when we started work. By now we are so used to the amount we have to do that we are able to finish by 11 am but do not go home till around midday. On the way to work two men left the Company and brought another cow to the camp. In the afternoon each of us received about 2 lb of meat as our share and we cooked it until midnight. It became cloudy towards evening and so there were no Russian aircraft about.

4 March 1945

We were supposed to leave today, but nothing happened. Instead, we were shown a new place where we were to work about half a mile. Each of us had to dig 4 yards of trench one yard deep. We could not dig deeper on account of the water coming up. In the evening the commander of the 8th Company ordered his men to get ready to leave, but they did not go anywhere.

5 March 1945

We continued to dig at the same place in the morning. Then at 3 pm, we were told to prepare to move and at 4 pm we left our camp. We walked about 5 miles and were then waiting for further orders on the side of the road between Altdamm and Stettin. It was not until 2 am the following morning that the order came to return to the camp, which we reached about 4 am. All the day and night the enemy were very active in the air.

6 March 1945

We got up at 8 am and left for work at 9 am. We could clearly hear the Russian artillery firing and estimated the distance at not more than 5 miles. The German artillery fired some ranging rounds into the fields around our huts. We expected the order to leave at any moment. We had some very greasy soup as we had eaten all the meat. In the evening it began to snow and the ground soon became white. We could see a great blaze of fires along the eastern horizon.

7 March 1945

We were woken early, 4 am, and told to prepare to move. After receiving 24-hour ration packs we began marching at 8 am. In the Stettin suburb of Altdamm we stopped to rest and dispersed in houses from which the occupants had been evacuated. Then we marched through Stettin where we saw a lot of ruined houses – the result of air raids. We arrived at Warsaw late at night, and were shown a barn with some straw where we could rest. Although it was very cold we slept well.

8 March 1945

Left at 2 pm to another suburb of Stettin which took us quite a while to find. We had to wait until dusk before it was decided where we would be quartered. At last, when most of the men had dispersed into nearby houses, Lieutenant Berzins[10] arrived and took the rest of us to a large room in a public house. We slept two to a bed and on the floor, while some of us slept on wardrobes which they had laid flat on the floor.

9 March 1945

Spent the morning washing, shaving and generally tidying up, and then continued to make ourselves comfortable at the pub. After dinner the Company Commander announced that someone had stolen a bottle of alcohol from the pack belonging to the commander of the 1st Platoon. The CO had decided to drill the company until the guilty person confessed. We had been drilling and running for more than an hour, when the Platoon Commander decided that he could not remember for sure whether he had drunk the bottle himself or not. Received ¾ lb of bread and soup in the evening.

10 March 1945

Left Zedlitzfelde at 7 am to work in Politz. It took a long time to find the place where we were to work, and the spades and picks, so we did not start work till 11 am. On the way we stopped at a synthetic petrol plant which had been almost completely destroyed in an air raid on 8 February.[11] We were digging trenches along the bank of a canal, while over the River Oder we could clearly see the explosions from a Russian rocket launcher. Finished work at 3:30 pm. Once more we received only ¾ lb of bread.

11 March 1945

I am duty NCO and stay behind. Around 11 am I could hear a powerful artillery bombardment not far from us. Boiled some potatoes, same as most days because the rations are not sufficient to keep one alive. An unexpected issue of smokes in the evening: 26 cigarettes, 1 oz of tobacco and 2 cigars, for which I paid RM 3.02. A clear and quiet night.

12 March 1945

The front line has been suspiciously quiet all day. A lot of Allied planes flew over us about 11 am, but we could not see them as there was thick cloud. We were working digging an anti-tank ditch. Several 'Todt' Organisation men were giving us instructions, and as a consequence a lot of the work was done twice over. In the end we left at 3:30 pm. According to rumours we are supposed to receive 1¼ lb of bread per day but actually receive only ¾ lb.

13 March 1945

We sat around for 1½ hours at place of work waiting for the tools to arrive. Rumour has it that all the tools have been taken by the men of the 'Todt' Organisation to Swinemunde, where they are supposed to be working on clearing the debris caused by air raids. In the end we were told to clear a space through a big pile of bricks where the anti-tank ditch is to pass through. Received in the evening 1¼ lb of bread and four herrings. According to rumours the Russians have been beaten back 7 miles from Altdamm. Foggy and rainy weather.

14 March 1945

We went to the site but did not do any work and sat around for two hours. Then we did a bit of training and arrived back by midday. According to rumours two Latvians have been hung in Politz for stealing. Received 1¼ lb of bread, and have been told that over the next few days we will be given the amount to make up for the days when we received short rations. In the evening thirty men are added to our company from the disbanded 4th Battalion. Foggy and a little rain.

15 March 1945
A spring-like and sunny day. We were each given a spade and worked until 3:30 pm digging the new anti-tank ditch. On the way to work, and later on the way back, we were ordered to sing which we did not like at all.[12] We had a singing lesson in the evening. The food situation has improved considerably and I have a couple of slices left over for the morning meal. After boiling some potatoes in the evening my stomach is full for the first time in a long while.

16 March 1945
Finished the anti-tank ditch and started on a new section. We could hear the sound of artillery fire from the direction of Stettin from 9 in the morning until after dark. A hazy but warm day. Rumours that a civilian has shot one of our men for stealing. In the evening Lieutenant Berzins lectures us about cleanliness and tidiness, but we are not particularly interested in his warble.

17 March 1945
We finished the anti-tank ditch, but have been promised a new place of work tomorrow. All day the weather remained cloudy and we had some rain. We found a potato store under an earthen mound quite near to where we were working, and everyone filled their pockets and food carriers with this exotic fruit. I had a shave and a good wash in the evening, as if to celebrate the weekend. There are rumours that we are only going to be given ¾ lb of bread a day, so the potatoes will be a great help.

18 March 1945
It is Sunday and we get back from work early, but only because we are working to a schedule. In the afternoon I washed some socks and towels and did some sewing. I also managed to have a good wash. According to rumours, the Russians have gathered a considerable force opposite Politz, and it is possible they will try to cross the River Oder here. The day passed quietly. Only a couple of the enemy's planes circled over our village.

19 March 1945
We have been digging an anti-tank ditch near Politz, right through an orchard. It seemed a pity to dig up the beautiful apple trees which the old farmer had planted himself thirty-five years before.

It was hard work because we struck water about 2 feet down. Although the ground was quite firm underneath, the water seeping into the ditch from the sides made work almost impossible. Again ¾ lb of bread.

20 March 1945
Although we were told that today we would have to finish the ditch that we started yesterday, this morning we began work at a different place where the ground was dry and the digging easy. A fine spring-like day, but I have a cold and have had a headache all day. Went to bed early in the evening; we had no electricity and I did not feel at all well. A clear night.

21 March 1945
We carried on with our work at the same pace, although the food situation has not improved – still ¾ lb of bread per day. I usually eat all my food in the evening and then manage without eating until the following evening. I have nothing to smoke at the moment. I still have a cold and my head aches every night. We have no medicine and the doctor can't even get me an aspirin.

22 March 1945
I've had a headache all day and don't feel like working. The day is clear and spring-like once more and there are green buds on the birch trees. Received ¾ lb of bread in the evening and then we were given some more – altogether 1½ lb. This was supposed to be the balance for the days on which we received only ¾ lb – the supposed daily ration being 1¼ lb. I managed to eat all the bread in the evening and immediately felt better – the whole world seemed a better place.

23 March 1945
A beautiful spring day. Having finished the anti-tank ditch we were free all day. I managed to sunbathe. We even felt hot on the way home with our greatcoats on. Rumours are that we are going to central Germany for training. 1¼ lb bread. They have saved about 1 lb of bread per man at the Company Supply Depot and have promised we'll be given it before we set off. This remains to be seen.

24 March 1945

In the morning we could hear the sound of anti-tank and machine-gun fire from the direction of Mesentin. The German artillery fired all day in the direction of the Russians. Finished work at 2:30 pm and went back. Tomorrow is Palm Sunday, and on account of this I had a wash and put on some clean underwear. We received some sugar and had the luxury of drinking sweet coffee. A clear warm day and night.

25 March 1945

The Germans have concentrated a lot of artillery in the forest around Zedlitzfelde which began firing early in the morning. A couple of Russian shells landed in the fields around our village. While we were digging the anti-tank ditch Russian shells whistled over our heads and exploded about half a mile behind us. Some of our men, the more timid ones, went to seek shelter in a dugout, but most of us just laughed and watched the shells explode. The weather is warm and fine, and the buds are bursting out on the trees around us.

26 March 1945

Continued to dig the anti-tank ditch. The Russians were quiet in the morning, although they fired about ten shells into Politz around 9 o'clock, which caused a great cloud of dust to appear above the town. In the afternoon Russian planes flew overhead, but none of them were hit by our anti-aircraft guns. The current rumours circulating in the company maintain that we will be leaving soon for central Germany, but there are counter rumours that we are to carry on working here.

27 March 1945

I am duty NCO and do not go to work. Made myself a rucksack from a blanket, and handed in my boots to the cobbler to be repaired. The Company did not return until 4 pm. The men told me that they had started to work at a new site further away. They had found some personal belongings buried by civilians, but were disappointed not to find anything worth taking. My friend Zeltkalns found some potatoes which we boiled in the evening. We could hear a lot of German artillery fire during the night, which was foggy. The 6th Company have had to work all the night.

28 March 1945

German artillery started firing early this morning and have kept it up all day, with only a few short breaks. The Russian guns have mostly been silent. Then, as we were on the way home from work, the Russians started to fire in earnest on a German battery by the roadside. One of the shells landed only about 20 feet from us but luckily no one was hit. The shells were of a large calibre and scored some hits on the Germans, besides breaking a line of high-voltage electricity lines. Our platoon was saved by the corner of a house behind which the shell landed, peppering the wall of another house with a row of splinters.

29 March 1945

Apparently we don't have much work left to do around Politz. We finished the anti-tank ditch today. The Russians bombarded us today with light artillery and a couple of times we had to take cover in a bunker. Most of the shells landing in the soft earth did not explode. One of them penetrated the bank of the ditch close to me but did not explode either. We examined the shells and found Latin letters on them, from which we concluded they were not of Russian manufacture, but were probably made in either Britain or America. The calibre was of about 10 cm and they exploded with a great noise when landing on a hard surface. The bunkers were large and strong. Built above ground for workers of the Artificial Petrol Plant, they had even withstood the Russian bombing from the air.

30 March 1945

Once more I am the duty NCO and remain behind. It is a peaceful day and even the Russians are quiet. We boiled some potatoes and made a meat sauce from a roebuck which had been shot by Kukedams.[13] The meat was very tough and we had a lot of trouble to make it palatable, but at least it filled our stomachs. In the evening there was a conference for battalion commanders, under the commander of the Regiment. The weather is damp and rainy.

31 March 1945

Working at a new site approximately half a mile from home. Although today is Easter Saturday you would not know it. We have been told that we will even have to work tomorrow. Did not receive any extra rations for Easter. Received only a rucksack, a pair of socks and a handkerchief. The rucksack is most welcome: until now I had nowhere to keep my belongings. Wrote a letter to Gaida in the evening.

1 April 1945

Easter Sunday today, but we continue to work as usual and have not received any extra rations. In the afternoon an officer passed on greetings from the Commanding Officer, and that was all. Our CO has managed to obtain a quantity of crude spirit from somewhere. This was diluted with water and issued to the Company. Each man received 4 oz and we felt just a little bit merry. Rumours that we would have to go to Schwerin for training.

2 April 1945

Working today as well. Knocked off at 1 pm and the afternoon was free. Changed to summer time today, and all the clocks are moved forward one hour. We are a little bit better off for food. The dinner time soup is thick, supplemented by potatoes bought by the Company. Zeltkalns has organized a daily supply of milk and potatoes. We have some meat as well. Kukedams has shot another deer today and we are boiling the meat until late in the night.

3 April 1945

Working as usual. It seems that we have enough work for two more days and then we will have to leave. According to rumours our destination is Schwerin, where we will do some training. There is a major attack by the British and Americans on the western front at the moment, and we are told that they are advancing almost unopposed for 30 miles every day. The distance between the British and Russian lines is supposed to be only about 300 miles.

4 April 1945

The weather is bad this morning. It is raining and there have been some hailstones. It is windy and cold when we continue our work making the bunker on top of a hill. The earth is clayey and the digging hard. We have been told that soon we will receive only ½ lb of bread per day, but I do not believe this. The Russians are not attacking for the time being, although to the west the British and Americans are supposed to be advancing rapidly. The minimum distance between the Allies is now supposedly 200 miles.

5 April 1945

The Company Commander has ordered us to finish the bunker today and we had to work until 3:30 pm to do so. We have to start work at a new site tomorrow so it seems that we will not be leaving for some time. In the evening we were given the opportunity to serve as paratroopers in a Special Duties Unit. There are rumours that the volunteers will be sent to Latvia, but I did not believe this and therefore did not add my name to the list. We are promised the issue of some smokes before 10 April.

6 April 1945

We continued to build the bunker. The weather was fine and sunny and I went for a long walk in the surrounding forests in the afternoon, during which I saw some deer. Kukedams has been lucky again today and has shot two bucks. Late in the evening we were told that we would not have to go to work tomorrow but that reveille would be at 7 am and we would be leaving. In the evening listened to the radio at Battalion Headquarters. All night the men were boiling potatoes of which they had accumulated large amounts. The night passed peacefully.

7 April 1945

Spent all day preparing for the march. Boiled our last potatoes and Kukedams cooked his deer meat in large canisters. The dinner soup was very thick, and in the afternoon the cooks boiled some potatoes as well. We received bread and food for four days and set off at 5 pm. We are supposed to be marching some 30 miles, our destination being Cracow. The day was fine and warm, but in the night it was cold and we had to sleep in our greatcoats. The road was comparatively well surfaced.

8 April 1945

BATINSTAHL, south of Stettin

We reached our destination as the sun rose in the morning. Some men had been sent ahead to requisition quarters for us, but they did not seem to have done their job. In the end we were quartered on a large farm where we had to sleep in a barn on some straw. There is a spirit distilling plant on the farm and therefore plenty of potatoes. In the evening I finished all my bread and boiled some potatoes. I was quite tired and soon went to sleep.

9 April 1945

The day began foggy and cold, but later the sky cleared and the sun shone. The digging is easy and we were back by 3 pm, although in the morning we had been told we would have to work until 7 pm. I boiled some potatoes and wheat in the afternoon as I had no more bread left. Heard some rumours that we have little work here and after a week we will be on the move once more. The British are supposed to have reached Bremen, about 175 miles from Stettin.

10 April 1945

Worked till 2 pm. There was some thick milk soup for dinner. In the evening I boiled some potatoes and felt for once as if I had had a decent meal. Tomorrow the Company is supposed to move to new quarters, about a mile from the farm. The Company has used its own funds to buy some potatoes and peas, and the commander is promising soup twice daily starting from tomorrow. They have even bought a cow. Took over as Duty NCO in the evening.

11 April 1945

The Company was roused at 5 am and shortly afterwards we left for the new farm. Here our platoon is quartered in the loft of an unfinished house. We made ourselves as comfortable as possible. We've been told that from 14 April we are to start receiving first-class food and also cigarettes. For our supper we had a thick pea and meat soup, made from products bought from the company's own resources. Each man was also given approximately ¼ pt of wine. We have managed to slaughter a cow today, and from this I managed to get 4 lb of meat.

12 April 1945

After finishing work today we had to camouflage the trench which we had dug the day before yesterday, and we did not get back until 4 pm. I sewed on a couple of buttons, then melted down some of the cow's fat and poured it in an empty tin. In the evening I read *Daugavas Vanagi*[14] by the electric light which our lads had managed to fix up. Around 9 pm we had our supper – a soup of peas and milk. A fine day and a clear night.

13 April 1945
Finished work by 2 pm and went home. We heard rumours that the President of the United States of America, Roosevelt, had died, and this was confirmed later. The British have moved a considerable distance and are nearing Berlin. In the evening each man received 1 oz of tobacco, some sweets, 2 lb of bread, 2 oz of butter and ½ lb of cheese. This issue is supposed to be in lieu of past shortages. In future we are supposed to receive 1½ lb of bread per day.

14 April 1945
The Germans told us in the morning that each man had to dig 4 yards of trench. Later our Commanding Officer arrived and amended that to 6 yards per man, besides which he ordered that we would have to work until 4 pm. There was a lot of discontent and complaining about this order, and the time was amended to 3 pm. Rumour has it that we are to leave here very soon. Otherwise nothing special. The food situation has improved and we have enough to eat.

15 April 1945
There was a strong frost this morning. The weather here is quite different from that of Latvia. Although the days are quite warm, the nights are cold. The apple trees have begun to blossom. We worked half naked in the warm sun today. More rumours that our work here is coming to an end. Nearly every day we receive either sweets, vodka or wine. The company's food supply is much better than ever before.

16 April 1945
I was twenty-one today. I did not celebrate it, but worked as usual; somehow the work seemed boring and the day passed slowly. I had to force myself to finish my allotted stretch of trench at the same time as the other men. The day is hot and hazy, but the night was clear with lots of stars in the sky.

17 April 1945
I was duty NCO and stayed behind. This duty is like a rest from work. I helped the company cook to mince some meat and later had a good meal in the kitchen. Received 36 cigarettes and 6 cigars in the evening. I had eaten too much during the day and suffered

from diarrhoea in the night. Around 11:30 pm a runner arrived from Battalion Headquarters with orders for us to prepare to leave. We got everything ready and went back to sleep.

18 April 1945
Slept until 8 am. Then the order came to leave in half an hour and there was a hurried issue of rations. We began to march around 9 am, rested for 1½ hours at dinner time and then continued on our way. We reached our destination at about 11 pm – Gegensee. We had marched around 35 miles. In the end we were quartered in the loft of some stables, and went straight to sleep because we were tired from the long walk.[15]

19 April 1945
We did not do much during the day, but spent most of it resting. We could not get hold of any news as all German broadcasting stations are supposed to be off the air. The Russian offensive began on 17 April from Stettin to Frankfurt am Oder in the direction of Berlin. In the evening each of us received 3 oz of rum, some margarine, cheese, sugar and four sweets.

20 April 1945
There were no orders to go out to work today. In the afternoon we had the ceremony of the Solemn Soldier's Oath, taken by those who had not done so before. During it a few aircraft approached and our Commanding Officer ordered us to take cover, but the planes turned out to be German ones. In the evening the Company Commander distributed 2 lb of pork per man for a payment of RM10. I managed to arrange for my piece of pork to be smoked and in a couple of days it should be ready.

21 April 1945
We were awakened at 5 am and at 6 am left for work. It rained right up to lunchtime and the work progressed slowly, so that it was 4 pm before we were allowed to go home when we had finished the allotted length of trench. We were wet through and very cold, but no one was bothered by it. Bought a knife off the cook for 2 oz of tobacco.

22 April 1945
Worked as usual, but today's weather is fine, the work goes well and we were back by 2 pm. Got back my piece of smoked pork, but the meat had not been salted and had become sour and smelly. We heard in the evening that a special company was being formed to guard the battalion.

23 April 1945
The names of the men posted to the Special Guard Company were read out this morning. My name was among them and so I did not have to go to work. Our commander is the commander of the former 5th Company, and my previous superior officer, Kubulins. We did not have anything to do until dinner time, and then the new company was paraded on the road. The commander explained our task and also announced that I would be his battle runner, and for the present would have to help the company clerk. Moved into the Company office.

24 April 1945
Worked all the day painting signposts for the new company and preparing personnel cards for all the men. The British and Americans have stopped all diplomatic communication with the Russians. But these are only rumours.

(From this point the 'on-the-spot' diary entries continue but are supplemented by fuller accounts written in the POW camp of Neuengamme in July 1945. To avoid duplication and confusion I have omitted most of the material contained in the 'on-the-spot' diary entries, except where it does not appear in the longer descriptions. *(LB)*

25 April 1945
The company left for training which I did not have to take part in. I therefore remained in the company office and continued to fill in the personnel cards. Later these were not accepted at Battalion Headquarters as they had not been properly completed.

I was alone in the company office when, around 9 pm, Kubulins arrived. He ordered me to go to the Company Supply Unit and tell them that we were to leave shortly. They had to go immediately to the supply depot and collect our rations. I announced the order,

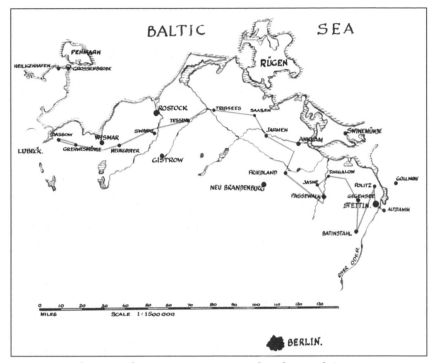

The march to escape capture by the Red Army.
26 April to 3 May 1945.

packed my kit and waited outside for the food issue, which was delayed for some reason. Outside it was a warm spring night. Russian aircraft were droning around the sky above us. They had dropped some illuminating flares in the direction of Stettin, where they hung like fairy lights just above the horizon. The civilians of the house where we were quartered had been told to leave early in the morning. They did not sleep either but were packing their belongings and also buried several suitcases in the orchard.

At last, around midnight, we received our 24-hour rations, this time an unusually large amount. We received bread for eight days, 2²/₃ of a loaf. We received less margarine and fats, for five days, also sugar, cigars and sweets. The men were joking, saying that this would probably be the last issue of food we would receive from the Germans. Later this proved to be true.

26 April 1945

Shortly before 3 am a runner arrived from Battalion Headquarters with an order for the Company to parade on the road in marching order, but it was 4 am before we started to move. No one knew our destination and various rumours circulated among the men of the company about this. At least our road led towards the west, away from the Russians, which pleased us. The weather was favourable: a cloudy sky and cool air made walking easy. We passed through several small towns where the inhabitants regarded the strange body of troops with amusement – about half of us were armed with spades, the rest carried rifles. The road led from Gegensee to Torgalow. About 3 miles before Torgalow we turned off the road and dispersed in a dry pine forest for a rest on the moss-covered ground. The Commanding Officer told us we were to remain here until we received further orders. This could mean tomorrow, I thought. After eating some of my food I took off my boots, wrapped myself in my groundsheet and went to sleep.

I was awakened by the shout to get up and prepare to leave at once. I had slept for two hours, the time was 1:30 pm and the march resumed at 2 pm. All day we could hear the sound of battle and the drone of numerous aircraft engines from the direction of Pasewalk. From the forest road we soon turned on to the Berlin–Swinemunde highway and there we met a stream of refugees going in the opposite direction. These people seemed to have escaped from Berlin. Among them we could see well-dressed men and women. We followed the highway to Jarmen where we remained in the street awaiting orders from Divisional Headquarters concerning our eventual destination. While we were there a large formation of bombers came over and unloaded their bombs somewhere outside the town which was well protected by anti-aircraft guns. At last our orders arrived, we left the town in the direction of Pasewalk and turned off the main road to the right. We marched another 3 miles and as the sun set reached a small village where we were allowed to make ourselves at home in the loft of a cowshed. Although I was tired from the day-long march I did not go to sleep straight away. I got washed and had something to eat first. The evening was warm and hazy, and a full red moon hung in the sky. When I did go to sleep in the hay I could hear the noise of Russian planes roaming overhead and during the night I was occasionally woken by their bombs exploding on the surrounding roads and villages.

27 April 1945

When I awoke the sun was already high in the sky. Our lads were busy killing chickens and pigs: the farmer had left everything behind when fleeing the place and we were preparing to have a good meal at his expense. We were constantly threatened by Russian aircraft which continuously flew over the village and bombed the surrounding roads and houses. For my breakfast I managed to obtain a mess tin full of milk to which I added some coffee and sugar. I also ate a couple of slices of bread. The rooms of the farmhouse were in great disorder – our lads had already looted them. I found an old-fashioned microscope which I decided to take with me, although its magnification could not have been more than 250 times. At about 11 am the order came to leave the village and take cover from enemy aircraft in the neighbouring forest. The cook and the Company Sergeant Major stayed in the village and continued to prepare dinner for the men, although there seemed to be little hope of eating it. Rumours were circulating among the men that we would have to leave shortly, and that the Russians were only a mile and a half from us. We could actually hear the sound of machine guns not far off.

At 2 pm the Sergeant Major and the cook were fetched from the village and we started marching. To start with, I helped to pull along a small barrow loaded with half a pig, from which I was promised a share, but after a while the barrow broke down and we had to throw the pig into a roadside ditch. Before leaving the others who were trying to mend the barrow, I cut off about 2 lb of fat meat, put it in my mess tin and followed the company. The weather was close and hot. Soon I disposed of my greatcoat and the microscope by throwing them into another ditch. We had to get a move on to put some distance between us and the rapidly advancing Russians. When we left the forest a short while later enemy aircraft were already attacking a road only a mile away – I could clearly see the bombs leaving the dive-bombers to explode on a crossroads overflowing with traffic. Our road led to Friedland, some 22 miles away. To start with we walked through a forest, but then came out onto a highway which was full of retreating German army units. Then we were hit by a sudden thunderstorm and the heavy rain soaked us to the skin. Luckily the sun came out again and we were soon dry once more. At last, around 11 pm, we were shown into a large cow shed on a farm, where we slept among the cows on the straw-covered floor. The farm was still some 5 miles from Friedland.

28 April 1945

We were woken at 5 pm and ordered to prepare to move. The Russians were supposedly following us along the road and only about 7 miles away. After passing through Friedland we began to follow a small country road in a northerly direction towards Anklam. According to rumours, the enemy had been stopped at Friedland and the new defensive line there, although we had not seen anything of this new front line, only a few miserable slit trenches.

We continued our march at an increased tempo with short rests until 4 pm, when after covering some 30 miles we stopped for a proper rest. We were quartered in a barn at the side of a road approximately 6 miles from Jarmen. The road was filled with an unending stream of refugees and soldiers, all heading west. Our bread reserves were rapidly diminishing and all of us tried to obtain and cook some potatoes and the meat we had organized on the way. I fried all my remaining pork, boiled a mess tin full of potatoes and after eating it all went to sleep. The night passed peacefully and I slept undisturbed until morning.

29 April 1945

Woke at 8 am. Others were still asleep, but those who had got up early cooked and boiled potatoes once more. We didn't think we'd be staying there for long, but the order to move did not come. Then, around 2 pm, a tank attack alarm was sounded. About half the company prepared to leave at once, while the second half took up positions on the eastern outskirts of the village.

At 2:30 we started to march in the direction of Jarmen, which we reached without a rest on the way, and did not stop until we had left the town 3 miles or so behind us. Here we met the Supply Units of the 15th Latvian SS Division. The carts in the column were overloaded with pigs, chickens and rabbit hutches, and the horses struggled to pull them along the sandy road. During the rest break Karnups[16] caught up with us riding a bicycle. He had remained behind with half the company which had taken up defensive positions at the village on the eastern side of Jarmen. We could hardly believe his tale. About an hour after we had left the village a patrol of two Russian motorcyclists had approached the village, followed by a group of enemy soldiers – some ten or fifteen men in all. Our lads had fired a few shots at the Russians and had then fled across the fields to join us. They had seen that with the approach of the enemy several white flags had been put out in the village, and at the outskirts of the next village the inhabitants had been preparing a flower-covered triumphal arch to greet the Russians. All this seemed unbelievable, but we knew Karnups and realized that he was telling the truth.

When we continued marching we saw several German aircraft near a forest clearing. One of the planes was burning and sending up a high column of smoke. It seemed that it had been shot down by the enemy. Very soon it became dark and we continued marching through the warm, fragrant, night. The people of the villages we passed through regarded us in silence. Once it was dark they disappeared, leaving us to keep marching into the night. According to our Commanding Officer we were heading for Saasen – some 22 miles. There we would have a rest for three or four hours before carrying on. A few men were sent off ahead of the main column to look for quarters. We could see the blaze of numerous fires all around us, except for a narrow gap to the west. We reached Saasen around 11 pm. The battalion was quartered in a barn where we could only sleep uncomfortably due to lack of space – it was quite impossible to move or walk about. We were forbidden to light a fire or smoke. One end of the barn was open and we could hear the drone of enemy aircraft.

30 April 1945

The battalion was woken at 3 in the morning and told to prepare to move. I felt very cold having practically slept outside. By now the blaze of fires could be seen all around us, even to the north and west – the direction we were taking. After passing through a large farm it became clear that the Russians had not been there yet. Several German aircraft which were dispersed in the fields of the farm were burning fiercely. The Germans were setting their own planes on fire, perhaps because they lacked the fuel to fly them. We continued marching along minor country roads without any proper rest breaks until 1 pm. Then, after marching about 25 miles we were billeted in a large farm by the roadside where we were told we could have some rest. The road passing the farm was packed with soldiers and civilian refugees heading west.

I put down my pack in a safe place and obtained some potatoes from a nearby store. I had already peeled the potatoes and was preparing to boil them, when all of a sudden the order came to prepare to move again. I left the uncooked potatoes in my mess tin, which I hung on my belt, then had to rush to the farmyard to collect my kit. We were told that Russian tanks were only 6 miles away.

We set off once more at 2 pm. The men were exhausted and several of them lay down by the road to rest, too tired to carry on the unending walk. After marching 10 miles the column neared Tribsees. We could see a white flag on one of the houses and there was confusion on the road. We passed through the village and continued on towards Tessin, which we had been told was to be our destination. During the march Kukedams talked a Pole into handing over a two-horse cart on which we loaded our packs and marching became a little easier. We were worried about the food situation. I finished off the last of my bread, margarine and sugar that day. All I had left was a little dripping and a mess tin full of potatoes, but I had no chance to boil the latter.

In the evening, we entered Tessin just as the sun set. We passed through the town and continued marching in a westerly direction. In the town several of our men managed to 'organize' bicycles. After marching another 5 miles we were allowed to rest in a barn. We had marched about 30 miles, it was nearly midnight and I was asleep in a moment. During the night we were joined by several of our men who had got left behind and had now managed to catch up.

1 May 1945

I awoke at 6:30 am. The morning was clear and sunny, and my first thought was to get something to eat. I boiled the potatoes I had peeled the day before, mashed them and added the dripping which I had had with me since the better days at Batinstahl. As soon as I had finished my breakfast the order to prepare to leave came and we set off at 8 am. Our destination was mentioned as being Gistrow. We were approaching the Neu Brandenburg–Rostock highway along a country road packed with soldiers and civilians. We could hear artillery and machine guns firing over to our left – the guns themselves were clearly visible only about 400 yards away slowly approaching the road junction. As I ran through a hail of bullets as fast as I could, I saw another Legionnaire lying face down in the roadside ditch, but did not have time to stop and find out if he was dead, or just taking cover. Then I had to run for another seven hundred yards across open fields, and was tired out when I reached the safety of the forest. I think most of our company managed to reach the same forest, but I was the first to get there. I was not prepared to remain close to the Russians for long and after a short rest I gathered a small group of men around me. Considering the possibility of capture by the enemy, we tore up our military passes and removed the SS insignia from our collars. Then I got out my compass and started to lead the group in a westerly direction through the forest. Beyond the woods we crossed a small marsh and in a village came across the cart carrying the company's packs, driven by Kukedams. He had managed to cross the highway just ahead of the Russian tanks. I found my pack and, without waiting for the rest of the company, started off with my group of men across the fields to the west.

We soon reached a railway bridge which we crossed just before German sappers destroyed it. They gave each of us a handful of cigars which they were distributing freely from a large tea chest. Once across the river we felt a little safer from the enemy and stopped for a short rest on a farm. Then we continued on our way to the west, led by an officer, and heading in the general direction of Wismar. In one of the villages we met the 1st Regiment resting peacefully. The men were surprised by our tale of the encounter with Russian tanks. According to them our regiment was still behind us, assembling in the small town of Swanne. We decided not to wait for the Regiment, and having obtained directions from the officers continued on our way. Before leaving the village we managed to get into a dairy where we could have had as much curdled milk as we wanted. At some stage in the confusion of the last few hours I had managed to organize a loaf of bread and I now walked along eating it, and drinking the curdled milk with relish. We passed through several villages and saw some French prisoners of war who we heard were allowed to go home already.

Towards evening we turned onto a larger road and even here we saw numerous white flags on the houses along it. As we marched in the direction of Wismar it became dark, but we kept on walking until, half an hour after midnight on 2 May, we reached our destination – Neukloster. Here we were billeted in a nunnery which had served as a hospital. I was very tired after marching non-stop 40 miles or so, took off my boots and went straight to sleep.

2 May 1945

I awoke when the other units which had arrived while I was asleep were preparing to leave. It was 4 am. I had great trouble getting my boots onto my swollen and aching feet, before staggering down the stairs and walking slowly across the yard. I did not join the collection of units of the Legion and the German Army, but found my own Company. We left at 5 am and marched off in the direction of Wismar. Although we were moving along minor country roads, we were still attacked by British and American aircraft. They fired their machine guns and rockets into the crowds and dropped small anti-personnel bombs. There were several Latvian families living in the surrounding villages – they had already escaped once from Latvia and were now packing their belongings once again to join the retreating soldiers heading west. We heard rumours that the Americans were not far away and were already in Gistrow. Around 2 pm we rested in some woods about 7 miles from Wismar, at the side of the Lubeck highway. I made a fire and baked some potatoes which I had managed to obtain locally. The men of the 3rd Battalion who arrived later told us that they had met Americans in Wismar. According to them the Yanks were quite decent – they had only taken away from them their bicycles and rings, and had searched them for watches. When we heard that the Americans were already behind us, our spirits improved considerably, and we continued marching at 6 pm, our fatigue forgotten. We passed through Grehwesmuhle, and in the rapidly gathering gloom we marched on towards our destination – Lubeck – which was indicated by the rays of our searchlights and the blaze of fires. In the end we did not reach our destination as the news spread through the marching column that all the bridges on this side of the town had been blown up. The battalion and company commanders went off to look for accommodation, and we were left by the side of the road. We waited for them to return for two hours, then Straupnieks[17] and I went into a village and lay down on the floor of a large cowshed. The next day we met the American forces and that evening were sent to the prisoner-of-war camp at Grehwesmuhle.

3 May 1945

We slept until lunchtime and then left in the direction of Lubeck. We met American tanks on the road, but managed to get to Dassow where prisoners of war were assembling, and that evening we had to go to Grimmen where the main camp was situated.

(Here the 'on-the-spot' diary entries end. *LB*)

Notes

1 I had fallen asleep on the train from Berlin and only woke up when it had already left the station and was in the marshalling yard. I had to trudge through thick snow back to the station, and then go to the barracks in the town where everyone was still up and playing cards. They had been waiting for the arrival of the New Year, Pommers was my friend from Riga where he lived quite near to our flat. At that time I still had a fine Panzer Grenadier's tunic from my service with Battlegroup Jeckeln. Grants and Ruze were my friends from the hospital in Czechoslovakia.

2 I managed to 'organize' the underpants at the hospital in Czechoslovakia during my Christmas leave. No one could manage on issued rations alone, and reference to this can only be seen as a forlorn attempt. Dealings in food and cigarettes were going on all the time, mostly among the soldiers themselves.

3 Rubauskis was my room mate from the hospital in Czechoslovakia. He was an ex-Labour service man who had been wounded near Iecava in Latvia. He still had a large piece of smoked ham from home in his ruck-sack, which we all used up gradually and which provided some of the food for the celebration on 18 November.

4 The camp at Polnowa was situated about a kilometre out of the village. There were two new arrivals at the Company, Zeltkalns and I. The Company Commander was 2nd Lieutenant Kubulins. When arriving at the barracks the Company Supply man issued each of us with a loaf of bread and a large piece of sausage, at the same time telling us not to mention this extra issue. Sleeping was in two-tier bunks and I got a lower bunk, near the stove, which was a good thing as the nights were cold and it was much warmer there. From the windows of the hut we could see an open field to the south with a low hill, but to the north, where there were no windows, the forest came right up to the wall.

5 *Junda* was the front-line newspaper of the Legion, and since leaving hospital Ruze had been working on its staff.

6 As long as the Company Commander could see us in front of the barracks, we did the prescribed training, but later we marched over the hill and, hidden from view, stood about in groups talking and resting.

7 Lans was the Company Sergeant Major at Paplaka in the autumn of 1943. On arrival in Russia I met him at the supply unit of the Company, where he had tried to rape the Russian woman. Later I had dealings with him during my stay in Russia and during the retreat in the summer of 1944.

8 The Company Commander Kubulins apparently came from Latgale –
I could detect a slight accent in his speech. He was particularly consid-
erate towards me and Zeltkalns, perhaps on account of our long
service with the Legion and our experiences on the front line. Both of
us had Iron Crosses, and it is possible that the CO hoped to have us
nearby in a tight corner. Most of the other men in the company
consisted of those who had managed to avoid being called up until
now, or were young lads.

9 Juris Zeltkalns from the parish of Skrunda. 'Sturmmann' and decorated front-line man. Arrived at Polnowa at the same time as I did and
we remained friends. Like myself, he commanded a section.

10 He was with me on the Chemical Warfare course in Riga 1943.

11 See diary for 8 February 1945.

12 Having been forced to sing in the Army, my father resolved never to
sing again, and he never did. (*LB*)

13 Janis Kukedams from the parish of Jaunpiebalga; he was our chief
poacher, who hunted in the surrounding forests.

14 A Latvian newspaper and also an organization for Latvian independence. The name means 'Hawks of the Daugava'. (*LB*)

15 One of our companies, which left after us, came under artillery fire
here from the Russians, who were crossing the River Oder on their way
to Berlin. The company suffered several casualties.

16 Karnups was one of the platoon commanders of our company, with
the rank of sub lieutenant. He was a middle-aged man. I later met him
in England during the Manchester or Bradford Latvian Song Festival
in 1954.

17 Jekabs Straupnieks from the parish of Nica in Latvia. He was the
Company Clerk. Artist-painter. I met him in England in 1952.

Part VI

Prisoner of War

Chapter 18

Prisoner of War, Summer and Autumn 1945

(Written from memory in 1963) 3 May 1945

It was quite late on a sunny morning when we woke up. As we came down from the loft of the cowshed we could clearly see that we did not have to hurry any more to escape from the Russians – we could see American soldiers driving past along the road to the east. They did not need to march like we had done over the last few days of the war. They sat comfortably in their lorries, chewing gum and smoking cigarettes.

We looked at the visitors for a while, ate anything that we still had left, washed our faces at the pump in the farmyard and then began to move slowly along the road towards Lubeck. We did not have to hurry any more and our feet were still tender from the long marches over the last few days. 'We'll be alright now,' everyone was saying. 'We'll get some good American food down us and will be able to rest properly.' The Americans did not take much notice of us, just waving us on to indicate the direction we were to take. Sometimes they dropped a cigarette or a bar of chocolate on the road for us. They even threw away half-smoked cigarettes, and we eagerly picked them up. We had not had a decent smoke for such a long time and wanted to try a new kind of tobacco.

Our destination turned out to be Dassow. When we reached the village we assembled in a field and were told to throw all our service equipment, weapons and maps in a heap. There was

187

another pile in the field where we had to throw all our knives. It was here that I had to part with the excellent knife I had acquired a short while earlier in an exchange deal with the cook. We could keep all our clothing, but I did not have much left in any case. Besides the clothes I stood up in I had a blanket and a German Air Force greatcoat which I had obtained a few days before while searching through a bomb-damaged supply column. I took the greatcoat because I had thrown my own away during the retreat. Later, in the POW camps, I was mighty glad for this coat as my only blanket was soon stolen from me.

That evening, escorted by American tanks, we began the march back to Grehwesmuhle where the first POW camp had been erected. On reaching the camp, an open field, in the middle of the night, we passed through the entrance proudly announcing that we were Latvian, naively hoping that we would receive special care and attention. But the Americans did not take any notice of us. They just shouted 'Yes, yes,' and 'Schnell, schnell,' the same as they had to the Germans, and waved for us to go to the middle of the field. We could not understand their indifference – we were their friends! We had tried so hard during the last few days to reach them. We even had ambassadors and consuls in America who, no doubt, had explained about our fight against the Bolsheviks. And they themselves would be fighting the Russians in a few weeks' time to free our country for us. This view seems to be stupid and naive now, but then we all believed that this was the only possible solution to our problems, and sceptics were soon silenced by logical arguments.

We stayed in that field for a couple of days. The Americans did not bother us and their guarding was perfunctory. A tank occupied each corner of the field with a sentry standing in the turret keeping an eye on us. During the night the headlights of the tanks were turned on and directed to the sides of the field, thus forming a fence of light. As for us, no one even thought about escaping – we were only too happy to have come through the war safe and sound. A large group of Latvians gathered in the middle of the camp during the first couple of days to celebrate their good fortune by drinking from a pair of milk churns full of crude spirit which they had managed to bring with them. There was a lot of singing and noise, but in the end the Yanks had had enough of it.

A group of armed Americans entered the camp and upset the churns, spilling the precious liquid onto the grass. Otherwise our captors hardly bothered us.

We watched black soldiers in amazement as they performed acrobatics on 'organized' bicycles whilst firing their weapons at some cows grazing in a neighbouring field. Very soon an understanding was reached between prisoners and guards, and a lively exchange started to take place. The prisoners supplied rings and watches for which the Americans exchanged tins of food, chocolate and cigarettes. We had not been given any food and most of us were very hungry after a couple of days' captivity. My first attempt to exchange a silver ring with Latvian colours and some SS insignia for food ended fruitlessly. It seemed that the Yanks were not in the mood for trading. When I approached them they turned a machine gun on me. I had to retreat and stay hungry a little longer.

I managed to exchange the ring a couple of days later for a few tins of meat. By that time we had been transferred to a new place, a couple of hundred yards from the original field, by the side of a lake. On the way to the new camp the Americans handed out the first food issue: one egg per man. We did not get any more food for ten days and that was only when a Supply column of the German Army was directed to the camp with its meagre reserves of bread, margarine and jam.

There were some trees and bushes at the new camp, but these disappeared within a few days. Although we had no knives, we managed to cut down the branches to make shelters and used the wood for making fires. In a short time the lakeside had lost all its trees. We destroyed the fresh green vegetation before the very eyes of the Americans like a swarm of locusts.

15 May 1945. Grehwesmuhle POW camp.

We were now separated from the main German camp, thoroughly searched and placed in a special camp. The Germans had told the American Camp Commandant that we were Latvian SS volunteers and, as such, merited guarding with special care. The food situation was disastrous. The normal daily issue consisted of about 5 oz of tinned meat and a cupful of soup. We had not had any bread for about a week, not counting the time we received one loaf between twenty-three men – that is a little over 2 oz of bread each. At the same time the Germans had received the same loaf for eighteen men. Our so-called 'leaders' (officers) did not seem concerned at this injustice. They were too frightened or incapable to insist on our rights, or perhaps they were too busy 'organizing' their own supplies.

On the whole our 'leaders' behaved in a curious manner. During the first few days of captivity they kept themselves apart from the men, but later, when they saw that we were ignoring them, they mixed with us again. They were used to giving orders and wanted to continue to do so, even here. As soon as the Americans recognized them as officers they began to form headquarters and other units. Some of the officers – the ones with Supply Units present in the camp – seemed to have plenty to eat, drink and smoke. Others, with no such resources, tried to obtain food and drink from their men's rations. The following case illustrates the situation perfectly.

A couple of days after being placed in the separate compound we were allowed to go to the Supply column and obtain our Company's supplies. The Germans had got there first and had taken whatever they wanted, so our lads followed suit and a lot of the rucksacks they brought belonged to the Germans. No one seemed bothered by this and it was decided to divide the contents of them amongst us. The officers thought that the food should be handed over to the kitchen, but we objected and tried to prevent this from happening. We knew that if the officers' recommendation was adopted most of the food would disappear into the bellies of the cooks and officers. One of the latter, stuffing his mouth with some cake he had found in a suitcase, resisted the soldiers' suggestions for a time. In the end, as the objections persisted, he had to give way and agree to the men's request for dividing the loot, which consisted of blankets, groundsheets, trousers, shirts and other clothing, while among the food there was bread, pork, jam, tinned meat and other good things. The food and clothing was eventually divided up among everyone.

The supply man from our 2nd Battalion was not there for some reason and so the rations were received by the man from the 5th Company, Buss, who took the lot to the commander of the 2nd Battalion, Captain Volbergs. There in front of his tent sat his batman dressed in blue fatigues. After putting down the bread and fats, Buss told the batman to look after them, whispered something in his ear, and went away to start dividing out the clothing and other minor items received.

After all the clothing had been shared out Captain Volbergs returned to his tent to oversee the correct issue of the food to the companies, or rather to see if he himself could get the lion's share. As the bread was being shared out an officer and several soldiers pointed out that one loaf was missing. Captain Volbergs was forced to recognize the fact and counted the loaves ten or more times, but it made no difference – there were still only six no matter how many times they were counted. Then the soldiers' attention turned on the unlucky batman who had sat all the time in front of the tent. He tried to make up another loaf from some slices and end pieces, but he could not do so as the total number of loaves issued to the Battalion had been $7^2/3$. I pointed out the fact that an aluminium tin containing some pork was also missing, but I was told to keep quiet by Captain Volbergs, who could not stop the flow of accusations against the batman. The men wanted to search the tent and to get rid of any of our officers who did not act in such an obvious case of stealing. Captain Volbergs did nothing to clear up the matter, but kept on counting the loaves which of course remained at six. At last the batman could not stand the accusations being made against him any longer and disappeared into the tent. A few moments later he handed out the missing loaf and after more shouting, the aluminium tin with the pork as well. The batman himself remained in the tent – all we could see were his legs sticking out through the entrance flap.

The men were now incensed and demanded that those guilty should be punished. But Captain Volbergs did not say a word to his batman, only shouted back to the crowd, 'You've got your bread and your meat, what more do you want?' and then continued to share out the food. A ginger-headed man was especially persistent and had a sharp exchange of words with a thin, pot-bellied officer. The officer kept asking the man his name, but the latter would not give it or stop shouting. In the end the officer, shaking with rage, promised to talk to the soldier in the morning and left the scene.

Gradually the noise and excitement subsided, and everybody received his share. It was true that the amount of food we received was small – approximately 1 oz of bread and a teaspoon of meat and jam per man – but the row was not over the quantity. The men wanted to prevent the officers and cooks from robbing them of their share of the food which they needed to keep alive and ward off hunger.

Evening came and everyone settled down for the night. Only the officer's batman kept going round the camp asking everyone, 'Do you know the name of gingerhead?' At last someone must have told him and he disappeared into his tent.

The next morning the Regimental Commanding Officer, Ritsik, called out Ginger by his name and gave him a stern talk about contradicting an officer. He was supported by Pot-belly. In the end the company commanders assembled their men and told them that the Americans fully recognized the officers and as such we would have to obey their commands. Anyone not conforming to this would be handed over to the Americans and shot. No one really believed this but there may have been some truth behind it and the soldiers dispersed, disappointed in not getting rid of their former commanders.

19 May 1945. Grehwesmuhle POW Camp.

It is the Saturday before Whit Sunday, quite different from others in my life so far. The company was woken at 7 am. Then, at 8 am, there was the morning roll-call during which I became so cold that I could not get warm until dinner time. The morning was cold although the sun shone, but a cold wind was blowing from the direction of the sea to the north. For my lunch I was given a thin sweetish soup of oatflakes. The food issue for today was as follows:

    Breakfast – tea, 5 gm
    Lunch – soup, oatflakes 2 oz, sugar
    Supper – soup, oatflakes 2 oz, milk 5 fl oz
    Bread and fats – bread 10 oz, tinned meat 5 oz

Men born in 1928 or after receive a supplementary issue of 4 oz of rye biscuits.

Washed my underclothes and socks in the afternoon. Rumour has it that the British are going to take over guarding us, and one of them arrived at the camp today. He was dressed in a Scottish skirt. I swapped a couple of pieces of soap for two rye biscuits – that was all I could afford to celebrate Whitsuntide.

*   *   *

We are all hungry, some more than others, depending on the character of the man. I do not feel too hungry in the morning up until dinner time. Only when I have received and drunk the pint of soup do I begin to feel hungry. Then I usually try to find something to do and thus keep my thoughts off food. I feel most hungry in the evening. After being given the bread and tinned meat I eat it all straight away, but do not feel satisfied by it. On the contrary, I feel more hungry than ever until I go to sleep.

22 May 1945. Grehwesmuhle POW Camp.

The guarding of our camp was taken over by the British on Whit Sunday. The German Commandant of the camp told the British that we were SS, and we were separated from the other camp inmates. We were placed in a field fenced in by barbed wire and with a searchlight mounted at each corner.

Yesterday a written appeal explaining our situation was handed in to the British Commandant of the camp and today the commander of our Regiment was called to see the British Lieutenant. The latter explained that he could not do anything about it. A British regiment is due to arrive within a couple of days and a commission will deal with our complaints. According to our commander, our case is supposed to be handled by the former Minister of Transport in Latvia, Blodnieks, at present in a Latvian Displaced Persons' camp in Lubeck. He had already telegraphed London and received a reply that within the next few days a representative of the Latvian government in exile would arrive here. We will not be handed over to the Russians in any case. Shortly before it fell, thirty ships left Courland[1] carrying soldiers and refugees, and they are interned for the time being near Kiel.

It rained all day and night and I stayed in my tent.[2] We have not had fine weather since the day before yesterday. A strong wind is blowing the sand across the camp. There is a lot of trade going on, especially with cigarettes, and the prices are approximately as follows:

Bread ¾ lb = 10 cigarettes = RM 200
Tinned meat 3 oz = ⅙ of a tin = 6 cigarettes = RM 120

4 June 1945. Neuengamme POW camp.

We had got used to the camp at Grehwesmuhle. We had sent appeals concerning our situation to the British Commandant and had been promised an answer. The food situation has gradually improved. The daily issue was equal to that of the German Army, maybe a little better. Suddenly, on the evening of 31 May, it was announced that we would be leaving for another camp on 2 June. On hearing this our officers told us that we would be with other Latvians and conditions would improve.

The morning of 2 June was fine and warm. We were woken at 4 am, took down our tents and set fire to the straw on which we had slept. Then, at 5 am, we marched out through the gate and set off for the station, leaving behind us the camp in the smoke and morning mist.

Marching through the small town we could see that the majority of the inhabitants were women, most of the men having died in the war or being in a prisoner-of-war camp somewhere. Although it was still early in the morning the women had begun forming queues outside the few shops, waiting for them to open. We halted near the station and were told that we would board a train, for which we would only be allowed ten minutes.

Our officers' batmen had the most trouble. The officers hoped to live at the new camp as comfortably as they had here and had ordered their batmen to take their tents with all their poles. Meanwhile the officers themselves carried their heavy suitcases with great difficulty and a lot of puffing and blowing. During their stay at Grehwesmuhle they had managed to arrange for their wives and girlfriends to come and live in the town, and the women had supplied them with food and clothes. Some of the officers had managed to save ten loaves of bread and a lot of other food. The men laughed and made fun of the overloaded batmen while their masters looked on with sickly grins on their faces.

A short while later the trains arrived, we were quickly aboard and were on our way. We had plenty of room in the cattle trucks – forty men per truck – and we set off in the direction of Lubeck. We could see the summer in all its glory – something we had not seen while living in our barbed-wire enclosure. We longed to be free and to live a peaceful life. We would have liked to have lain down in the green grass, but even when the train stopped our British guards would not let us dismount even for a moment. We did not stop at Lubeck, but passed south of it and were soon heading westwards along the main Berlin–Hamburg line.

We stopped in a Hamburg suburb around 1 pm and were immediately told to get off the train. The next order was to throw away all tent poles and pegs. Some men had to give up their personal musical instruments. Then, closely guarded by British soldiers, we began the 3-mile march to the special SS camp at Neuengamme. The weather was hot and close, we were forced to march at a fast pace and I was quite tired when we reached the camp. No one appeared at the windows of the houses by the road. We knew there must have been people inside as each house had a list of inhabitants pinned to the door, so it seemed that they had been forbidden to look.

We reached the camp at 3 pm. It was a large camp built during the war by the Germans for Russian prisoners of war. First of all we were lined up on the square, split up into companies of 250 men and searched several times. We had to hand in all knives, scissors, any tools, maps and compasses, and service watches. The searchers also helped themselves to personal watches as well. At last, around 5 pm, we were released and allowed to go to our barracks. Each company of 250 men had to elect a company commander and an assistant. We were also told to select another man to be in charge of collecting and allocating our rations. Each company was divided into five platoons, each with its own commander. The rules for the camp were very strict, our daily schedule was as follows:

7 am	Reveille.
7:30 am	Morning roll call lasting about forty-five minutes.
9 am	Parade of working parties and men needing medical attention.
11 am to 12 am	Dinner time. Some companies were given their soup at this time, others received it in the evening.
5 pm	Issue of bread and other food.
6:30 pm	Physical exercises and showers.
8:30 to 9 pm	Evening roll call and lights out.

*   *   *

The roll calls were held as follows: the companies lined up on the square in ranks of five and then a British officer walked past them counting. The reports were made in German, but the commands were given in Latvian. The evening roll call usually did not end until 9:30 pm. There were twenty-six companies in all, each of 250 men, which meant that the total number of prisoners in this camp alone was around 6,500, of which approximately 1,500 were Latvians. There were several such camps in the neighbourhood. There were rumours that this was only a transit camp from which we would be sent to work for two or three years in France or Britain.[3]

The food situation, on the whole, was no worse than at the previous camp. At lunchtime we receive about two pints of soup made from turnips and containing some fat. The bread issue varied from 9 to 10½ oz per day. The issue of tinned meat is around 4 oz daily. We did not get any tobacco or cigarettes and this was our main worry. The price of one cigarette fluctuated around RM40 and 2 oz of tobacco cost about RM1,500. As I had only RM11 in cash I could not even consider such a luxury as smoking.

On the day of our arrival the officers were separated from us and quartered in special barracks. We were not allowed to talk to them, but that did not worry us – quite the opposite. Most of us were glad to be rid of our former commanders. When sharing out the rations it was now impossible for the officers to take the lion's share as they had done in the previous camp. The soup and other food here was prepared in a common kitchen, so it was impossible for the officers to be given more than their due. On the whole I liked the life here much better than at Grehwesmuhle. We lived in wooden huts and it was possible to get washed at any time of the day. It was hoped that the food situation would improve in time. I did not think that we would be moved from there for a while, and if the number of people remained constant, then it might be possible to organize the supply of food better.

(Written in 1965)

Neuengamme had, in fact, been a notorious Concentration Camp during the war and many Russian prisoners of war had died there. The main camp consisted of a large square surrounded by wooden huts and some brick buildings. A high barbed-wire fence enclosed the whole complex and there were also watchtowers in the corners. The washrooms were well equipped and their walls were decorated with murals painted by the former inmates. These showed the various occupations of the prisoners, who were dressed in striped concentration camp uniforms with numbers on their backs.

The discipline was very strict and offenders were punished near the main gate where the British sentry could keep an eye on them. There were two main methods of punishment. The first one consisted of the culprit being made to kneel on sharp gravel while holding a brick in each hand above his head. After a couple of hours the man could hardly walk. In the meantime he was rifle-butted by the sentry every time he dropped a brick. The second kind of punishment was being made to stand half naked in the hot sun with one's hands up, and again the sentry used his rifle butt freely if the hands started to droop. These punishments were only for minor offenders, whereas serious offences merited the man being taken away from the camp to the guardroom where he was locked up in cells. The treatment there, according to rumours, was far worse than the punishments meted out in the camp.

We lived in wooden huts which was much better than at Grehwesmuhle where we had been in an open field. There were not enough bunk beds for all the men, but this did not worry us unduly. Those without beds, and I was one of them, slept on the floor. Our officers had been separated from us on the first day so the newly elected company commanders were senior NCOs, and the men liked them much better than their former bosses.

When I first arrived at Neuengamme I had several maps of Latvia, among them an excellent motoring map, and during the initial search I had somehow managed to keep them. Later, on seeing the fate of men who had been found to have possession of forbidden items, I had to get rid of the maps. Quite often the British guards made snap searches of the prisoners and I had no inclination to risk my skin.

24 June 1945. POW Camp Neuengamme 2.

We had been at the first camp in Neuengamme for about three weeks and had got used to the life there. The days passed in idleness slowly waiting for the next meal. The food situation improved gradually, and yesterday each of us received 1¼ lb of bread and 1 oz of butter for the first time. It seemed that the reserves of tinned meat had run out as we had not received it for some time. The soups were getting better and thicker, and were made with pork. Sometimes we were even issued with two helpings of soup a day.

Rumours started to go around yesterday morning that in the evening we would have to go to another camp, from which we would be sent to Canada. We went to the next-door camp at 5 pm but were still there in the evening and had to celebrate the traditional St John's Night there. We all hoped that we would not be kept there for long. It was supposed to be a transit camp from which prisoners were being sent away every day. We thought that we would have to go to work, and without guards.

27 June 1945. POW Camp Neuengamme 2.

Several days passed, but we were still there. There was no suggestion that we would be sent anywhere in the near future. It seemed that the majority of Latvians were being assembled there. Only yesterday the few Latvians who had been left behind in the first camp with German units arrived. There were several British commissions active in the camp, and we thought that it would be the turn of our company to appear before one of these.

The amount of food issued each day was not large, but by now I had got used to it and did not feel too hungry. Each day we received around ¾ lb of bread and 2 oz of butter or margarine. Besides this, early in the morning we received one pint of bitter coffee, two pints of thin soup around 11 am, and one pint of sweet tea at 5 pm. No one seemed to be smoking. All the issues of bread and margarine fetched only six or seven cigarettes on the black market. The price of one cigarette was RM50.

8 July 1945. POW Camp Neuengamme 2.

The fine dry weather of the first days at this camp were gone. For more than a week it had been cloudy and the rain kept on falling, turning the brick kiln yards into a muddy morass. We were in good spirits during the first few days, hoping for release soon, but this hope was gradually fading and the food was becoming worse. The soup had become thin and for several days we had received only one loaf of bread per five men. Until now the same loaf had been issued to four men. Today, after a long time we got thick noodle soup and a quarter of a loaf of bread. Yesterday each of us was given two cigarettes for the first time here. In the afternoon we were visited by representatives of the Latvian Red Cross, who told us that everything was being done to help us. According to them this was one of the strictest camps in the district. They had asked for permission to see us several times, but only now had been allowed to do so. At other camps the regulations were not being so strictly observed and they had been able to send food into them for the prisoners, while it was forbidden here.

12 July 1945. POW Camp Neuengamme 2.

Life in the camp dragged on without any changes. Yesterday a Belgian unit took over guarding us from the British. Most of them were young lads.

Latvians who go out of the camp every day on working parties managed to establish contact with a Latvian Displaced Persons Camp, which meant that it was now possible to send out letters and receive parcels. We also had a list of Latvian civilian refugees living in the neighbouring camps. On 9 July I wrote to a family named Caune, thinking that they were perhaps the same family who lived at the railway station of Platone[4] where Mr Caune was the stationmaster. I received a reply and a food parcel yesterday. It appeared that these people were complete strangers, but the parcel was most welcome. It contained a loaf of bread, 3 oz of margarine, ¾ lb of salt, ¾ lb of sugar and ¾ lb of soup powder. I managed to eat all the bread and sugar with the daily issue until tonight which meant that in one day I had eaten five times the normal ration of bread.

And yet I did not feel full. It seemed that we had lost all sense of proportion as far as eating was concerned.

For the last few days the food, which had been the worst for some time, had improved somewhat. For four days running we were also given cigarettes and small cigars. All sorts of rumours were circulating in the camp concerning our release, but no one could seriously believe these any more.

I sent off letters to the following people today: the Caune family a letter of thanks, and to Gaida from Madona. I expected replies within a couple of days.

(The diary and notes written in 1945 end here.)

The second camp at Neuengamme was next to the first one and the former inmates had worked here. One half of the camp was occupied by a block of brick kilns and the rest was a field. We were housed in the brick kiln building and slept on the concrete floor, just in front of the kiln doors through which we could see the cold dark interiors. The weather was warm and we were not too uncomfortable lying on the thin covering of straw. We were very hungry and within a few weeks the leaves on all the plants growing in the field were gone. The prisoners cooked these in empty food tins and consumed the green stew with relish. There was a flourishing black market in food and cigarettes in exchange for almost anything one could offer. Due to the limited supply of food and tobacco, the prices were very high.

We were still guarded by a unit of Belgian soldiers, some of whose countrymen were inside the camp; they were Belgian SS volunteers. When the time came for their return home to stand trial for the crime of collaborating with the Germans, they were afraid to go. The guards had to search the whole camp and use force to assemble these prisoners and send them on their way.

Once, when we were all assembled in the field for the evening roll call several buses arrived at the gate and men in naval uniforms entered the camp. They were French sailors who had been on a sightseeing tour of Germany and the concentration camps. Some of them were drunk and all of them, as a result of their tour, were in an ugly mood. They walked around the silent POWs, shouted abuse and kicked the defenceless men. Our guards did not protect us, we dared not protest and had to endure the kicking with clenched teeth. When the Frenchmen departed no one was seriously hurt, but nevertheless we were morally degraded by this treatment.

A couple of weeks after our arrival at the second camp at Neuengamme the Latvian civilian refugees from the surrounding camps heard about our predicament. Two young girls were the first to approach the fence. This time the guards looked the other way and the girls threw over a couple of loaves of bread. One of these landed in the ditch and sank in the stinking mud, but we soon found it, washed the mud off and ate it with relish. The same loaf yielded something more valuable as well. Concealed in the middle of the bread we found a short note which gave a list of the names of Latvians in the neighbouring DP camps, and asked us to write to them giving our names. In return the civilians promised to send in food officially, through the Belgians, which was only possible if they knew our names.

After this incident, parcels of food started to arrive officially through the camp administration and were carried in unofficially by working parties. At that time the civilian refugees had plenty of food. Unlike us they were considered by the military authorities to be people who had suffered at the hands of the Germans and were amply supplied with everything they required. I used this opportunity, as did everyone else in the camp, and this way we obtained a lot of food besides our rations. But we were still never free from hunger. We had been short of food for a long time and needed more time to recover. On one occasion we were visited by a party of Latvian Red Cross workers and a vicar. The latter seriously asked the assembled prisoners how many of us, as a result of our suffering, had passed on to richer pastures. After a short uneasy silence someone answered with a straight face that we did not really know, but there must have been many. In fact we did not know of anyone who had actually died of hunger. After distributing a little food and a few cigarettes, the party departed promising to do everything possible to help us.

The time passed slowly but surely until near the end of July 1945 we were told we would be transferred to another camp. The day we were to leave Neuengamme we returned to the first camp for our final roll call. We prisoners were made to stand outside a wooden hut waiting our turn to go in. The door was guarded by a vicious-looking Belgian and each of us was pushed or thumped by him as we passed through the door. Inside the hut were a couple of tables with Belgian officers sitting behind them. Displayed prominently on the tables we could see the officers' pistols and whips. One by one we had to approach the tables, stand to attention and call out our name which the Belgians checked from a list. We were asked in broken German whether we had volunteered for service with the Legion, the answer invariably being 'No'. After this short examination we were allowed to leave the hut by another door, and pushed by another guard on the way out. Outside, the prisoners were crowded into a small yard guarded by Belgian soldiers who ordered us to kneel or crouch down in the hot sun – anyone moving was prodded by a bayonet or received a blow from a rifle butt. It took a couple of hours for all the Latvians to pass through the hut and then we had to wait for our transport.

I do not know what the purpose of our theatrical release was – perhaps the Belgians hoped to frighten some of us into confessing to being volunteer SS men. There were tales circulating later that someone, just as a joke, had answered 'Yes!' to the officers' question, and had been sent with us just the same. Some of the prisoners said they had been made to undress and their arms scrutinized for the tattooed blood group which the Belgians considered as conclusive proof of being an SS man. Most of us Latvians were released from this special POW camp with only a few remaining behind, and were released a few months later.

After walking through the gates of Neuengamme we had to board British army lorries and a short while later the convoy, escorted by armoured cars, moved off in a northerly direction. The journey through the green countryside lasted for about three hours. On reaching our destination we were greeted by other Latvian prisoners of war who were to show us our new camp. They told us that we would not be fenced in any more.

After gathering our few belongings we began to walk towards a wooded hill which hid the camp. It was only when we started to climb that we realized how much strength we had lost at Neuengamme. Resting on the way, we finally reached the top, then walked through the established camp where we were shown a couple of large marquees in which we were to live. Being tired from the unusually active day and the long journey, I left exploring the new camp until the next day, and went to sleep early.

I spent most of the next day walking in the country surrounding the camp at Putlos. There were several concrete bunkers near our marquee which the German Army had used for training purposes. Even now, on a large plain on the other side of the camp, one could see German tanks which the British Army had used for target practice. There were many fields of potatoes and ripening corn in the neighbourhood. As I walked I cast a speculative eye on the potatoes, but each field was guarded by German police and Latvian Legionnaires. I walked as far as the sea and could see a dark streak of land on the horizon – Denmark. Parallel to the sea was a row of Stone Age barrows which showed that man had camped here from the beginning of time. Even here, a few miles from the camp, the fields were guarded.

I stayed at Putlos for about five weeks, until the beginning of September 1945. We were once again under the command of Latvian officers and only saw the British when they inspected the camp. Anyone without documents was issued with a temporary Soldier's Pass and we even received our army pay in German notes, which were still valid.

In spite of the strict orders about stealing from the fields and the German guards, the prisoners managed to get the potatoes. There were cases when armed guards chased Latvians from the fields in full sight of their cheering comrades. One ingenious digger had found a piece of armour plate in one of the bunkers and pushed this in front of him between the rows of potatoes. The Germans fired several shots at him but the bullets bounced off the shield and the Latvian escaped arrest. The prisoners even managed to kill a sheep right under the nose of a German shepherd. As the flock passed one of our tents the men simply grabbed one of the sheep, pulled it into the tent and slit its throat. The Latvians also gathered near-ripe corn from the fields, dried it in the sun and then milled a coarse flour for cooking into a kind of thick porridge. The corn was milled by grating it in simple devices fashioned from empty food tins.

At Putlos we could receive parcels from outside without any restrictions; we could also to leave our camp altogether and live

204 Stormtrooper on the Eastern Front

with the civilian refugees in their camps. Most of the Legionnaires with relations in the Displaced Persons camps left Putlos as quickly as they could. As soon as the civilians had supplied them with clothes, they could walk out of the camp without any difficulty. Those remaining in the camp were without relatives in Western Germany, and even they hoped for release in the near future.

All the time I was at Putlos there were rumours circulating concerning the coming war between the Western Powers and the Russians. To us such an outcome seemed inevitable. We could not imagine the Western Powers allowing the Communists to continue occupying our own and other Eastern European countries.

Towards the end of August the rumours of our approaching discharge from the camp increased. Then, quite suddenly, one day we were told to prepare to leave for another camp. Before we boarded the train we stayed the night in a small transit camp near the station, where we slept in British army tents. Here I was visited by a woman from one of the Latvian families which had been sending me food parcels since Neuengamme. She had even brought some civilian clothes with her which I could use to leave the camp. I thanked her but declined her offer, believing that I would soon be released; I also did not think it very wise to leave the ranks illegally at the last moment. Thus, full of hope, I boarded the train and started the journey to an unknown destination in the first week of September 1945.

The journey was uneventful apart from two incidents. First we met some Russian prisoners of war returning home from Germany. Our former enemies had decorated their locomotive with the Red flag, and shook their fists as a parting gesture. Then, when we entered Belgium the people did not seem to like us either. Men working in fields made gestures as if cutting our throats and shouted incomprehensible abuse, while the women put out their tongues. These incidents depressed us considerably. Many of us started to think that maybe it would have been wiser to leave the train at Lubeck where the Latvian civilians had urged us to do so.

The first thing I noticed when the train stopped was the high barbed-wire fence enclosing the new camp. Then I saw some

Latvian POWs who were dressed in British army uniforms with a dark round patch on their backs and on one knee.

Before we were allowed into the camp we were searched and medically examined. Once more the doctors seemed more interested in looking for the tattooed blood groups under our arms than in our physical condition. After we had been liberally sprinkled with DDT delousing powder, we were finally released into the barracks. Thus started my stay at Zedelghem POW Camp in Belgium.

In the beginning life here was not too bad. The morning after my arrival we were given a good measure of thick white porridge with prunes. The dinner soup was thick and had plenty of meat in it, the bread was white and the issue of margarine, cheese and jam was sufficient. We were quartered in brick-built huts, sleeping in three-tier bunk beds. Every day we had to attend two roll calls at which the British counted us to make sure that no one had escaped. New trains bringing more Latvian prisoners arrived nearly every day until the camp was full to capacity. I met many of my old comrades here, men I had not seen since Russia and had imagined to be dead.

With the increase in our numbers the quantity of food issued per man diminished and soon we were hungry once more. It was getting colder with the approach of winter, and damp, foggy weather made us shiver every time we had to leave our barracks.

Besides roll calls we had to go outside every morning while the floors were being swept. I usually went out for a while in the afternoon as well, and walked around the camp a couple of times. First I would watch the black marketeers doing their trade near the wire separating the first cage of the camp from the second, then I would pass the kitchens and smell the tempting aroma of cooking. After walking along the perimeter fence under the watchful eyes of the guards in the towers, I would reach the open space at the end of the camp, turn and make another round trip before returning to my hut, No 89.

We had a stove in the middle of each hut, and this was kept going all night, but we were still cold and had to sleep fully dressed. By day nearly everyone did something to pass the time and keep one's thoughts off food. Many prisoners used empty food tins to make various boxes and cases. Others manufactured cigarette holders from toothbrush handles. Notebooks were made from the liberal supply of toilet paper which was of little use. The real craftsmen were the fellows who made 'gold' rings from brass. The camp had been an ammunition store for the Belgian Army and it was comparatively easy to find empty cartridge cases which the 'jewellers' used for their wares. The brass rings were polished with extreme care and, as a finishing touch, a hallmark was engraved on the inside. These rings fetched a good price when sold to the guards.

We did not get any cigarettes or tobacco at all until Christmas. In January each man received 500 cigarettes. This was a great help for everyone in overcoming their hunger pangs. Smokers felt less hungry and non-smokers could exchange their cigarettes for food on the black market. Some men, endowed with strong characters, saved their cigarettes and even managed to increase their stocks in various ways. These men, when finally released from the camp, had suitcases full of cigarettes and used them in Germany to start dealing on the black market – the budding entrepreneurs of the future.

During my seven months stay at Zedelghem I wrote a couple of times to the Latvian Red Cross enquiring about my mother and sisters. The answers were negative and I had to assume that they were still in Riga and under the rule of the Communists. We were actually quite well informed about life there. Some specialists in our hut had constructed a wireless set and early every morning we listened to the news from Latvia. Of course, we did not believe the rosy picture portrayed by the newscaster. All of us knew the Communists too well. The Russians came to the camp several times trying to persuade us to return home. The majority of us, however, were not deluded by these emissaries and the results of their appeals were negligible.

All of the prisoners were becoming thinner daily as time marched on. The only healthy looking individuals were the cooks, the interpreters and, of course, the black marketeers. With the coming of spring 1946 the weather became warmer and we welcomed the return of the sun after the cold, dark winter (with tremendous joy). Some days the sun was warm enough for us to sit outside on the earth banks surrounding each hut. As we soaked up the sunshine, we felt much better for it, our spirits improved and once more we hoped to be released soon. This time rumours became reality.

One day I was called before the Discharge Commission, and a couple of days later, on 25 March 1946, boarded a train for Germany. My adventures with the Latvian Legion had finally come to an end and I was being moved to a Displaced Persons camp along with many other Latvian refugees.

I stayed later in DP camps at Grossenbrode and Hamburg, from where, in late 1947, I arrived in Great Britain.

Notes
1 The peninsula in north-west Latvia which remained free of Russians until late on in the war.
2 I lived with two other men in a tent made from a length of cotton material.
3 This proved to be true.
4 The nearest station to the family farm in Latvia.